THE WORD MADE FLESH

The Word Made Flesh

The Meaning of the Christmas Season

KAROL WOJTYLA
(Pope John Paul II)

Translated by Leslie Wearne

1817

Harper & Row, Publishers, San Francisco

Cambridge, Hagerstown, New York, Philadelphia
London, Mexico City, São Paulo, Singapore, Sydney

FIRST EDITION

Designed by Don Hatch

Library of Congress Cataloging in Publication Data

John Paul II, Pope.
   The word made flesh.

   Translation of: Discese dal cielo, being the Italian and first-published version of homilies originally delivered and transcribed in Polish.
   1. Christmas sermons. 2. Advent sermons. 3. Catholic Church—Sermons.
4. Sermons, English—Translations from Polish. 5. Sermons, Polish—Translations into English.
I. Title.
BV4257.J6413   1985   252'.61   84–47738
ISBN 0-06-064203-3

85   86   87   88   89   HC   10   9   8   7   6   5   4   3   2   1

Contents

Translator's Preface

The homilies in this volume were preached in or around Krakow between 1959 and 1978 by the man who is now Pope John Paul II, but who was during that period Auxiliary Bishop and then (from 1964) Metropolitan Archbishop of Krakow. They are all concerned with some aspect of the mystery of the Incarnation, starting with the Annunciation and continuing through Advent, the Christmas season, and Epiphany, to finish with a selection from the Octave of Prayer for Christian Unity. Most of them were given in the much-loved, historic Krakow Cathedral, although a number were preached in other churches in the diocese—and some even in the open air on the site where he and the parishioners were struggling to obtain government permission for the construction of a church for a huge new industrial suburb.

They were preached over a twenty-year period, so that they provide us with clear evidence of Karol Wojtyla's unchanging emphasis on the importance of the fundamental Christian truths and values, his deep devotion to the Mother of God, and his constant stress on the centrality of the Eucharist. He often speaks of the various pressing problems of his diocese and country—atheistic education in schools and universities, the effects of the stresses and strains of modern life on the institution of marriage, government encouragement of abortion, and so on—so that we are provided with practical examples not only of his deep pastoral concern for his flock but also of how he never loses sight of the importance of applying theology and ethics in every sphere of individual and community life. We are given a demonstration of his wide-ranging pastoral, theological, and social concerns, and also, for instance, of the development of his commitment to ecumenism and Christian unity during and after the Second Vatican Council, in which he of course took part.

* * *

The homilies were selected by Father Carmelo Giarratana and Sister Maria Grzesiuk from the Polish typewritten transcriptions produced by various faithful members of the Diocese of Krakow. The present English translation has been made from the edited and abridged Italian version of Father Giarratana and Janina Korzeniewska, which was published by the Vatican Press in 1982 under the title *Discese dal Cielo* (*He Came Down from Heaven*); however, the Polish original has been consulted on a number of points.

English lends itself less to a rhetorical style than do Polish and Italian, so that I have had to simplify certain turns of phrase, eliminating repetition where this was used simply for emphasis. Since the present text will be read, rather than spoken out loud, I have tried to produce a text that reads more easily and is therefore slightly more literary but that still retains some of the immediate flavor of the spoken language.

As concerns specific points of translation, the main difficulty is with the word *czlowiek*, which is usually translated into English as *man*; however, in Polish (as in, for instance, German) this word has no sexist connotations and is not the same word as that used for *man* as distinct from *woman*. I have translated this word variously according to context as *the person* (in places where there was no risk of philosophical confusion), *human beings*, or simply *we*; even so, I have often used *man* or *mankind*, where any of the other choices appeared overly clumsy.

I have used the Revised Standard Version of the Bible for Scripture quotations, occasionally taking a word or two from some other translation in order to fit in with the Polish version used by the author. All the footnotes, and also the majority of the Scripture references in the text, have been added by me.

L. W.

1

The Feast of the Annunciation of the Lord

"And the Word became Flesh." These words from Saint John's Gospel have for centuries formed part of the Creed. Today on the Feast of the Annunciation of the Lord, the whole Church genuflects when reciting the words "and was made man" in order to emphasize its profession of faith in the mystery of the Incarnation of the eternal Word, the Son of God, from its very beginning.

There is also another occasion on which the Church genuflects when saying these words, and this is at Christmas, the feast of the mystery of the birth of the divine Son in the Bethlehem stable. "And was made man."

The two feasts of the Annunciation and Christmas are closely linked, with the second revealing what began in secret in the first.

With deep awareness of the mystery of the Incarnation in which the Word became flesh, I should like to consider the Son's words to the Father: "Lo, I have come to do your will, O God" (Hebrews 10:7, 9). Here we find the depths of the mystery: becoming man and thus sharing in our human nature, the Word places himself within human history as an offering to the Father in a perfect and absolute sacrifice against which all future sanctity will be measured. As gift of self he places himself within human nature, which is sunk in the darkness of sin and disobedience, the result of the removal of the human will from the holy will of God. He places himself as gift within the womb of a virgin. Mary is immediately aware of the depths of the meaning of what is to happen to her and exclaims: "Behold the handmaid of the Lord. Let it be to me according to your word."

The Annunciation to the Blessed Virgin took place in great simplicity, and the Church celebrates it without excessive pomp. Even so, it was a very important event. Although it may not have appeared particularly spectacular, it was so deep and so imbued with the central truths of our faith and expressed our relationship with the Lord so deeply that we should mark this feast with deep meditation and reflection on what this occasion has to teach us.

"Lo, I have come to do your will, O Father," says the Son, and "Behold the handmaid of the Lord; let it be to me according to your word," echoes his virgin mother. These words capture the mystery of the Incarnation, the beginning of that Redemption through which man's spiritual world is brought into balance and sin is redeemed right from the start, from our earliest ancestors down through the ages, including our own, to the end of time.

My dear brother priests who have come here today to celebrate the fortieth anniversary of your priesthood, you have chosen today's feast to gather around the altar as you did with your bishop, our unforgettable cardinal*, when you received your priestly ordination from his hands. You did well to choose this feast, because the priesthood constitutes the continuation of the mystery of the Incarnation and the constant fulfillment of the words which the Son of God spoke when he became man: "Lo, I have come to do your will, O Father."

These words were spoken in the wider context of the sacrifices of the Old Covenant that were no longer pleasing to the Lord inasmuch as they neither fulfilled his request for love nor expressed a perfect offering. Thus, from the very moment of the Annunciation and his conception, Jesus Christ, in becoming man in his mother's womb, gave expression to that which constitutes the basis of your lives, in other words, the priesthood. The priesthood in fact means offering God, as Creator, the creation and in particular humanity,

---

*Adam Stefan Cardinal Sapieha.

but, even more, offering him, as Father, that which only the Son can give.

This is the nature of the priesthood that was indelibly inscribed in you at the moment of your ordination and that has made up the tissue of your life, vocation, and mission throughout these forty years. Today you have come here in pilgrimage and prayer to commemorate and renew this priesthood.

You want to express your gratitude to the Lord for your priestly life. However, since you are aware that this gratitude can never be full enough, you entrust your words of thanksgiving to God the Father and Creator into the hands of Christ, his Son, to whom you are bound through your priesthood for this earthly life and for all eternity.

You too, my very dear religious sisters, have done well to take advantage of this opportunity to come here on pilgrimage. The mystery of the Incarnation and Redemption is also inscribed in your souls—in a different way from the mininsterial priesthood, but just as deeply, so that it entails just as much commitment. Your whole lives are an offering—a total gift of self, a full renunciation, in the spirit of the heavenly beatitudes, in accordance with which you seek to take as your sole model Christ himself, the incarnate Word, in his self-giving to the Father.

Self-giving is your secret, my dear priests and sisters. All Christians are in fact called to share in Christ's priesthood and mirror his total gift of self to the Father and to be a spiritual sacrifice; however, your lives express these elements in a special way and act as a sign for the whole people of God.

You have therefore done well to choose today's feast to come on pilgrimage to this cathedral to be with the Bishop of Krakow in order to commemorate the mystery of the Incarnation, which is the beginning of our Redemption.

Another reason why this is a wise choice is that this is a Holy Year. May this year of special redemption and reconciliation become a source of unceasing special graces for all of us who are gathered here in this cathedral, this shrine of our history.

25 March 1974

2

❦

The First Sunday of Advent

Let me first say a few words about the meaning of the Advent season that we are entering this Sunday and that marks the beginning of the liturgical year.

In the first place we obviously need to consider its historical (or, if you prefer, chronological) significance. Advent carries our minds back to the first human events, which also marked the starting point of the history of salvation, which led to Christ. Advent is the equivalent of this historico-chronological period of waiting for his coming and also of the unfolding of the mystery of Christ—in the first place of the Incarnation—inasmuch as this season brings us back to his hidden origins.

However, we can find other meanings in Advent. In the structure of Christianity it can be taken as indicating the deepest level. Christianity is the religion of the coming of God, of his breaking through into human history and life—an aspect which makes it stand out from other religions.

Islam is undoubtedly a religion of God's presence in the world as Creator; it is a religion of transcendence. The religions of the Far East, which are religions of the absence of God, are also, in quite a different way, affirmations of his absolute transcendance.

Maybe we need such affirmations so that awareness of absolute transcendence, which mystics possess in the fuller sense, can be communicated to us who live in faith in the Lord's coming, in that coming which is a fact. Faith encounters the historical fact.

After these introductory remarks, let us give further consideration to two phrases from today's liturgy, because they can help us to live this Sunday in a more interior way.

The first is the invocation, "Let us go with joy to meet the Lord," which the Church purposely places at the very beginning of the liturgical year. Let us go with joy to meet Christ. This describes the atmosphere of the mystery of the Incarnation and of Christmas, and also that of the period of waiting for him, which the Church enters on the first Sunday of Advent. All this finds its meaning and confirmation in each one of us. We all know that meeting with our Lord is the source of joy in the emotional sense of which Christmas and Advent tradition is full. However, it is chiefly so in its true, existential sense, according to which the greatest joy is everything linked to its end. And for the human person the end is the encounter with God. The person matures, is purified, and reaches self-realization in this encounter. All the uncertainty of our existence, which has its own built-in limits and is also limited by its actual situation, recedes only in the meeting with the Supreme. This is our hope—our eschatological hope. Eschatological hope is verified along the way, so that we can state that the Church's call to go with joy to meet the Lord hides a deep meaning. A child looking forward to Christmas in his own way can identify with this call, just as an adult who has experienced many things can.

The second expression I want to consider from today's liturgy are the words of the Apostle Paul: "You know what hour it is" (Romans 13:11). When everything seems to be turned to the future, so that we are almost torn from the present, the Church uses the apostle's words to bring us to a halt, almost as if it were saying: "Advent is the present moment: not tomorrow, but today; not later, but now." And what deep truth there is in these words!

This makes Christianity the religion of the Lord's coming, inasmuch as, while waiting for the Lord's coming, we actually experience it. His coming unceasingly fills and satisfies our "now."

Thanks to this factor, we live with the hope of eschatological fullness; we live Advent not only in the perspective of the liturgical year, but also in the perspective of the entire existence of the individual, each nation and all humanity. The moment which we are living and which we must "know" is maybe very similar to the moment described in today's gospel reading (Luke 21:25-33), so that it too gives rise to much reflection, some of it deeply pessimistic and fearful of catastrophe. We are right to wonder about the forms our civilization or world should take and with it the Church, to which through its past it is so deeply bound and of which it is the expression. We also considered such questions (although not always explicitly) in the course of the recent synod of bishops on evangelization.*

However, these reflections would carry us far afield to theories about the world and its evolution, and, even though such matters may be of deep concern to us in a different way, we must leave them in order to return to the simplicity of the word of God which calls us today, just as it has done for centuries, to go with joy to meet the Lord. This is a deep truth, both because of its simplicity and because of its clarity—and maybe not only for the believer but also in a certain sense for each person who seeks it.

I would urge you to strive to "know what hour it is," because this hour is also the time of the Lord's coming. Indeed, since God came each hour has been full of his coming.

My dear brothers and sisters, I should like to take the invocation from today's liturgy as the key phrase for our gathering, since every meeting is in a certain sense such an "hour." Let us try to understand its meaning and see how it can be full of God's coming.

I think that if we begin like this we shall be able to receive from this first moment, this first day of Advent, the sanctifying fruits of grace which are destined for each one of us and for us all as a specific community in this specific age. Let us pray for this while participating in the eucharistic liturgy.

30 November 1974

---

*The Fourth Synod of Bishops was held in Rome in October 1974 to discuss the subject of evangelization in the modern world.

3

The Second Sunday of Advent

Let us listen to God's word; thanks to the liturgical reform, we can savor its full richness. We respond joyfully to each reading we hear: "Glory to you, Lord. Praise to you, Lord Jesus Christ." Praise for the word, for the truth it contains and for the love with which you have proclaimed it to us; you speak to us without cease, and we listen to you without cease!

We listen to your word and recognize in it the simplest, but also the deepest, realities and truths. In the word of God for the Advent season our human situation is reflected very clearly. And if the key word of this season is "Come!" it is only the second aspect of this situation. We could say that week by week and day by day these Scripture readings which the Church offers us indicate that man has a sort of advent structure, inasmuch as waiting is a deeply rooted aspect of his nature.

This has many ramifications: it means that man is not sufficient unto himself, nor does he find his fullness in any specific historical period; and it also means that, following the deepest call of the heart, man feels the need to go beyond himself.

Today's liturgy speaks to us very insistently of the various meanings of this advent structure when it reminds us of those narrow, winding paths and those ravines, valleys, and hidden places that are found in each of us and that then expand on the level of society to become more and more serious.

The special feature of the Advent liturgy is that it traces a very realistic picture of humanity, inasmuch as, humanly speaking, it sees us as almost at the limits of despair and impotence. Despite this the picture also contains a great deal of light because of the fact that we have an advent structure, changing everything about ourselves with the invocation "Come!" and because we believe in our own self-realization and in our capacity for perfection and happiness. Believing in all this, we bear witness to the call which God addressed to us at the beginning.

Advent means God's coming as found within each individual and all humanity and also God's coming for which the individual and all humanity make constant preparation. These aspects are found in this present moment as we live it and also in every other moment in the history of salvation. Both aspects are always present: God's coming, which has already taken place and is recognized in the person, and God's coming, for which we make constant preparation—the coming toward which we move and to which we open our hearts, following the deep call we feel within ourselves and which we perceive through our spiritual sensitivity.

If, remaining within the liturgy of the word announced to us in Advent, we wanted to define the purpose of today's gathering, I would say that each one of us has the task of discovering within himself and others the advent structure of the human person.

In the second reading the Apostle Paul speaks about this point and about our mission and the mission of all Christians; and the Second Vatican Council, referring to these or similar words, stated that through its very nature the Christian vocation is a call to the apostolate. This statement is of great significance.

In the course of today we shall reflect on some of the specific implications of the fact that there is an apostolate of the laity. At the beginning of this meeting I want, therefore, to turn my attention to the primary meaning of this statement of the Apostle Paul and of Vatican II that expresses the age-old teaching of the Church, in other words, that the Christian vocation is, through its very nature, a call to the apostolate.

Seen against the background of today's liturgy and that of the whole of Advent, this means that each Christian must not only discover his own advent structure but must also help others to discover it in themselves. This task is sometimes even more difficult today—if only in appearance.

Maybe it is in fact easier under other aspects. In any case, the discovery of this structure in oneself and in others can be seen as the basis, precondition, and starting-point of any apostolate. The person must understand how incomplete he is in order to desire fulfillment and feel the need to go beyond himself. Then he calls out "Come!" and in this way rediscovers himself in that order of things that has its source in God—in the Most Holy Trinity—in the mysteries of creation and salvation. And we can be certain that if we say "Come!" he will come. God comes even when we do not call him and even when we are not thinking of doing so, because he knows that we call out even in silence.

My dear brothers and sisters, please take this brief reflection on the advent mystery of man as the start of the time we are to spend together and which we place on the altar here as an offering. Let us pray as we pray in every eucharistic liturgy that he who has already come may offer us as a gift to the Father; may he offer us and also this day of encounter which we dedicate to the service of the people of God and the Church of Christ in our country.

6 December 1970

4

The Feast of the Immaculate Conception

We cannot meditate properly on the Immaculate Conception of Mary, the Mother of Christ, if we do not bear in mind the true meaning of the term we are using. *Conception* means the beginning of human life and is not limited simply to the biological or bodily aspect but concerns also the spirit created by God at the moment when the parents generate a new body. The spirit constitutes the soul of this body or organism—the basis and the source of all life and of all those elements characteristic of the human person. The conception of a human being is the beginning of existence for a new spirit, and here we find the basis for understanding the meaning of the Immaculate Conception of Mary. Every human spirit could have begun in the state of sanctifying grace; in other words, it could have shared in the divine nature from the first moment of its existence and possessed a real capacity to participate in the interior life of God. The essence of sanctifying grace is in fact the divine life as grafted into the human soul, and if we do not understand this, it is impossible to view the Immaculate Conception correctly. The supernatural mystery of grace forms the immediate context for gaining an understanding of the privileged condition of the Mother of Christ.

We know from revelation (and there is no other way of knowing anything about this subject) that, as a consequence of the original sin of our first forebears, every person is conceived without sanctifying grace; it is this lack that forms the essence of original sin. Thus God creates the spirit to be the soul of the organism that begins its existence, but he does not bestow grace on it. In other words, at the moment of conception he does not give it a share in is own nature nor the capacity to take part in his interior life.

The human being therefore begins his existence far from God, without the strength of the supernatural bond. This strength will be given to him later by redemption, which is for all of us the source of grace and the basis of salvation—the grace and salvation which we lack at the moment of conception. Mary, on the other hand, possessed sanctifying grace right from the beginning, and we are reminded of this daily by the phrase from Saint Luke's gospel, "full of grace," which we recite at the Angelus.

The Immaculate Conception thus means a special crystallization of grace and supernatural life within Mary's human soul. Like each of us, Mary owes this grace to the redemption wrought by Christ. However, whereas it comes to every other person to free him from original sin and help him to overcome its consequences with a view to salvation and to union with God, it came to Mary in a different way: redemption anticipated and prevented original sin in her.

So if we want to meditate correctly on the Immaculate Conception we must see it in the perspective of the redemption brought about by Jesus Christ, man and God, the Son of Mary—and it is this last factor which explains why she was redeemed in a different way from the rest of us. Through the laws of nature, a son feels a special duty toward his own mother. Mary's Son, who was our Savior, fulfilled this duty perfectly; he redeemed her in a special way and in a special way gave her that grace which redemption unleashes for all of us.

Let us now reflect on what has been said about the Immaculate Conception especially in the context of holiness. Holiness is one of God's attributes and is identified with his essence, whereas it is not identified with the essence of human beings. Man is not holy by nature. (The theory of man's natural perfection, as advanced by Rousseau, is in constant conflict with both interior and exterior experience.) Even so, man tends to see it as the highest human aspiration. Naturally only a philosophico-religious perspective can link man's holiness to God. While it is true that holiness is normally used as referring to a high moral perfection or a certain heroism of life, only a living relationship with God gives it its true character as holiness. It is difficult to talk about saints except in the context of religion, and even the word "saint" belongs to the language of religion.

How are saints formed? For the moment we shall consider this question solely in relation to the mystery of the Immaculate Conception. Since sanctity is an attribute of God and is identified with his very essence, saints are formed by sharing in this essence and in the divine nature. Grace means such participation and is the basis of sanctity; in other words, it is sanctifying grace. However, since grace is a fruit of redemption, it links saints very closely to redemption. A saint is thus a person who in a special way benefits from the fruits of redemption. Now since the Immaculate Conception means the presence of sanctifying grace from the first moment of conception (a privilege exclusive to Mary), we do not hesitate to recognize her as a special saint, addressing her as "Most Holy."

Another aspect of holiness is that it is the fruit of heroic effort and struggle. This is where the concept of sanctity encounters the mystery of original sin, which leaves traces in the soul that are not immediately wiped out by grace but grow gradually fainter in proportion to how we cooperate with grace, although they remain in the soul in the form of tinder for the fires of sin (*fomes peccati*). In other words, although original sin per se is wiped out in the first grace we are given in baptism, its consequences do in a certain sense remain.

This is why sanctity, which is obtained as a result of redemption, takes form as a fruit of both grace and effort. This is the form in which we know it and in which it is seen and appreciated by all of us because it requires effort and because it represents the fruit of an interior struggle against the three lusts of the eyes, the body, and the spirit (this last referring to pride of life). In each of these lusts there is a type of natural inclination that hides a certain good; however, the inclination is distorted and disordered. Hence the need for interior struggle with ourselves, to which is added exterior struggle, since the world in which we live and move is full of the consequences of original sin: every human being is subject to sin, and the world is made up of human beings.

People become saints through the working of grace, which is the fruit of redemption. A great deal of its energies, however, is directed towards overcoming the consequences of original sin and neutralizing that tinder which is always threatening to catch fire—if not in us, then in others, in whole societies and in humanity as a whole! Thus the main function of grace (*gratia sanans*) in our spiritual life is that of purification, which must be complete before real inspiration and union with God are possible. If there had been no original sin, human sanctity would have been formed differently; and, indeed, in Mary, who was without it, it did in fact come about differently.

We are accustomed to viewing the formation of sanctity within man in the perspective of the consequences of original sin, and we tend to see its negative side, the struggle against the self, as a substantial and characteristic aspect, and this is to a large extent correct. However, only "to a large extent," since the struggle against the self is not the aim but simply the means of reaching the aim, which is represented by the full development of love (the most authentic outpouring of grace). Original sin brought a serious negative factor into the whole process of humanity's sanctification through grace. Mary's sanctity had to be free of this factor inasmuch as it had to be exclusively positive. However, we are so accustomed to the negative aspect that its absence is almost an irritation, which is why we find it so difficult to picture and describe Mary's sanctity. Contemporary writings give particular emphasis and a great deal of space to the negative aspect of holiness—to the element of struggle—so that it is seen almost as the principal measure of heroism, even though it is admitted that love is even more heroic.

Mary's sanctity is basically founded on her Immaculate Conception, a privilege which she obtained through her Son. Thus her sanctity is different from that of other people, who come to it through and despite original sin. Mary was redeemed differently and became holy differently, even though her holiness did come from sanctifying grace. Although she became holy differently, this does not mean more easily. When considering the sanctity of Mary in the context of the privilege of the Immaculate Conception, people may sometimes think that it was easy for her to become holy inasmuch as, since she was free of original sin and its consequences, she did not have to struggle against the three lusts. This way of thinking reveals a clear symptom of the conviction that the purifying function of grace is the sole or highest one and that the struggle with the self is in a certain sense the aim (or synonym) of sanctity.

Mary became holy more easily only in the sense that she was spared the struggle against the latent tendency to sin. However, she was not spared the labor connected with holiness and the herioism that is inevitably linked to it—labor and heroism that were found not in the struggle with herself as a consequence of original sin but rather in her active participation in the redemptive work of her Son. The gospel gives us clear evidence of this, describing difficulties that were peculiar to Mary's holiness and were comparable only to those of Christ himself. The holiness of Christ was also difficult, even though from the very beginning he had the fullness—and not only the subjective fullness—of grace, a fullness linked to the divine person of the Word-Son and to his universal mission as Redeemer. Nobody would dare suggest that his sanctity was easy, even though it had none of the elements of struggle with the self, which is what constitutes the negative aspect of holiness as it forms and develops in man despite original sin.

Mary's holiness, and the whole process of her sanctification, must be viewed in the framework of her complete and active participation in the redemptive work of her Son. In her, the forces of grace were not directed (or at least not to any great extent) toward overcoming the consequences of original sin and to struggling with the self in the sense I have just discussed; she used them, instead, in order to link herself personally, with her whole life, to the work of redemption.

The role of co-redemptrix (*alma socia Redemptoris*), which is recognized as proper to the Mother of Christ, gives us a new and more complete way of understanding the mystery of the Immaculate

Conception, inasmuch as this was not simply a privilege of the Mother of God-become-man but also anticipated the role which the mother would carry out alongside her Son. Her holiness therefore had to be different, just as it was difficult and heroic in a different way. Another person who would have had to devote a major part of the supernatural energies given by grace to the struggle with the self would never have been able to concern herself in such a perfect and universal manner with other people's redemption as was required by the vocation of the mother of the Redeemer.

In the sense in which we have considered it, the mystery of the Immaculate Conception has explicit reference to the interior life and formation of the Christian. Above all, the close link between the privilege (for the Immaculate Conception does undoubtedly represent a privilege) and the task or mission of Mary in the Kingdom of God has great importance. From this viewpoint the objective structure of the divine economy becomes clearer: there is a basic logic—an invisible, but nonetheless deep, reflection—of life and action in the work of redemption. Even though in its essence grace is a gift of God, human life and in particular man's supernatural destiny are a clear and logical consequence of the sublimity of the gift and of the exalted nature of man's tasks and missions.

When we reflect in this way on the Immaculate Conception of the Mother of Christ, we are indirectly considering our own lives and the role of grace in them. Religion cannot be simply a cultural element added on to the rest of life; rather, it represents a universal commitment to bringing about the Kingdom of God.

8 December 1959

5

❦

The Third Sunday of Advent

Each year on this third Sunday of Advent we hear the words addressed to Jesus by the messengers sent by John the Baptist: "Are you he who is to come, or shall we look for another?" (Matthew 11:3). The Church wants us to hear this question in Advent, since this is a period of waiting and of coming. Humanity waits for God, for Christ, asking: "Are you he who is to come?" This question, which was asked by John's contemporaries two thousand years ago, has been asked by each successive generation and is still asked by people today. We Polish bishops who took part in the World Synod of Bishops held in Rome, recently had confirmation of this. The subject considered by the synod was the evangelization of the contemporary world, and by listening to each other's experiences, we could see how contemporary men and women, no less than those of two thousand years ago, constantly ask Jesus Christ the same question: "Are you he who is to come?" This applies to contemporary people of every culture, race, continent, and economic or political tendency.

We are well aware that in a different way our own people of Poland also ask this question, despite the automatically expected reply that denies Poles the right to ask about God or seek Christ. This may be why people in this country feel a deep, even if confused, need to ask this question, if only within their souls or consciences. It is, indeed, the most important question in the history of the human race and cannot be stifled within the soul since it concerns the meaning of human life on earth, which cannot be sufficiently explained through means furnished by scientific or technological progress. The reply is given to us neither by the West nor by the East. Indeed, the more people claim to be giving the right answer, the more man will ask in his torment, "Are you he who is to come?" and turn his gaze on Christ.

My dear brothers and sisters! Faithful of the Diocese of Lódz! Today, the pilgrimage that has brought Our Lady of Jasna Gora to your parishes comes to an end. In the course of these blessed months we have seen many people in Lódz asking this question once again. And many have found an affirmative answer: "Yes, you, Jesus Christ, Son of the Virgin Mary, have been sent to save us and to give meaning to our earthly pilgrimage. You are he who is to come, and we do not look for anyone else."

Today, before the icon of Jasna Gora, we can state that Mary has made it easier to ask this question and that she has above all helped many of our brothers and sisters to reply from the depths of their souls and consciences. May she be praised for this! Her maternal spirit, which is far greater than any ordinary human spirit, has brought us closer to God and united us directly with him; she, as the Mother of God, is closer than any other person to him and more closely united with him in the kingdom of heaven. We cannot find words to express our gratitude to Our Lady for the response of faith which she has inspired in so many souls in Lódz in these past months; nor can we express the gratitude of the Bishop of Lódz and of the clergy, religious, missionaries and all the lay people of this diocese.

The pilgrimage of Our Lady of Jasna Gora to your diocese has taken place in the course of this Holy Year, which the successor of Saint Peter announced as a time of special renewal and reconciliation for the whole Church, and I think you should be particularly grateful to Mary for helping you to fulfill these hopes so effectively. For when a person is converted and finds Christ in his conscience and soul, then the worthy aims set for this Holy Year become fact. And this is what has taken place in your diocese in these months. Mary has moved among you, just as she moved through the life of

Christ and the history of the Church, silently and discreetly, and in doing so, she has helped you toward spiritual renewal and toward reconciliation with God and yourselves. May she be praised for this! And this is why, in the name of us all, I repeat the words of the archangel: "Blessed are you among women" (Luke 1:28).

During her visit, the Diocese of Lódz has sought with her to bring the Kingdom of God into family life. You chose this as the most necessary and essential task, and you were quite right. There is no more important problem today in Poland—indeed, we could say in the whole of Europe or in the world. The many requests addressed to the Holy Father both prior to and during the synod to take the family as its main theme go to show this. There is nothing more important for us in Poland than a family which is healthy, united, and strong in God. You were right to choose this task and to pray to the Most Blessed Virgin to help you to strengthen your families spiritually. And we have great need of help! A healthy and united family springs from sacramental Christian matrimony in which the partners vow to preserve love, fidelity, and conjugal honesty until death. Thus anything that impairs our conscience and social behavior constitutes a danger for the family and impedes its development. Even those who propose and try to spread a concept basically in conflict with Christian values agree on this point: the only healthy, united, and strong family is the one that accepts both the responsibilities of parenthood and those of providing a proper education for the children. These responsibilities are closely linked and in fact can be said to form one single task that involves every member of the family. The family, which you took as your principal focus during the pilgrimage and for which you prayed to Our Lady for help, is the foundation of the life of human society and of that of the nation, the Church, and the whole of humanity.

It is a great blessing that in the course of her pilgrimage Our Lady has, on your request, been able to play a role in this task. She has undoubtedly brought many couples, parents, and whole families closer to the Kingdom of God, in which love, fidelity, and conjugal honesty come to fulfillment, together with the indissoluble family community, which is the cornerstone on which future generations depend. I see it as a guarantee that during this pilgrimage a number of families have consecrated themselves to Mary, and I pray that not only now but throughout the future she may help them to bring the Kingdom of God into being in their midst.

Now that this holy pilgrimage is drawing to a close, our thoughts turn to the "fertile land" hymned by the prophet Isaiah in today's liturgy and also to the labor of farming as emphasized by Saint Paul in the second reading. The apostle says that in his labor the farmer needs patience and perseverance. And if we may address a prayer to Our Lady of Jasna Gora on this last day of her pilgrimage in Lódz, a city of factories and workers, let us pray that she may give us the patience and perseverance of the farmer:

We pray that you may grant us perseverance—you who have made our land fertile and our souls fertile in love, you who have brought us closer to Christ and helped us to find the answer concerning the meaning of life, you who have entered into our families. The Kingdom of God is brought about through patient and persevering work. Mother of Christ, Queen of Poland, our Mother, be an unceasing source of inspiration for us in the grayness of our daily labor. Help us to overcome the shortcomings and weaknesses that affect us to such a great extent. Help us not to lose sight of the task of human formation and spiritual development.

Today Our Lady of Jasna Gora is leaving your diocese and will continue her pilgrimage to other areas, churches, and communities. Together with the other bishops of the Polish Church who are gathered together here, I want to pray to the Most Blessed Virgin, our Queen and our Mother, that she may visit our fellow citizens and help them find the right answer.

We pray that you will help them to be converted and reconciled with God and with themselves. We pray that you may help them to overcome their weaknesses: help them all, both young and old, to overcome fear and to have courage. May the words of your Son to John the Baptist reecho throughout the land of Poland: "What did you go out into the wilderness to behold? A reed shaken by the wind?" (Matthew 11:7). May these words act as a warning, so that the wind does not bend us. We pray to you, Our Lady of Jasna Gora, Queen of Poland, to take our Polish souls, baptize them in the name of your Son, and accept and treat them with maternal love as you have done with so many souls here in the Diocese of Lódz.

We hope that the other stages of your pilgrimage may be as fruitful as those in the Diocese of Lódz and in the other places already visited.

Blessed are you among women and blessed is the fruit of your womb, Jesus!

15 December 1974

6

The Fourth Sunday of Advent

In the Advent season we hear the words: "I am the voice of one crying in the wilderness" (Matthew 3:3). We know that the forerunner of the Savior, John the Baptist, described himself in this way, thus distinguishing himself from "him who calls." In other words, he did not mean to identify himself with the one whose voice he claimed to be; and when they came and asked him, "Are you the one or should we wait for another?" he stated very explicitly that he was the voice of the other.

The call to make straight the paths of the Lord is the principal theme of the Advent call which rang out on the banks of the Jordan through the voice of John the Baptist. Many people in Israel, from every social class and walk of life, heard this call and came to ask how they should live; so we can say that that voice which cried in the wilderness, the voice of Christ's forerunner, was undoubtedly compelling.

The celebrations here today in the parish of Myślenice for the blessing of three new bells call to mind these Advent words. Bells are simply voices, and thus their importance lies in making the voice of God ring out and spreading it with their sound; they act as the voice of God which speaks, the voice of Christ which calls.

The three new bells of the parish of Myślenice announce and must transmit to the whole parish the Advent call first made on the banks of the Jordan by John the Baptist: "Make straight the paths of the Lord."

In the life of the Christian community, bells have a special role in that they speak to hearts and consciences. The power of this voice has been proven many times. It is a blessed voice (and this applies to the one we are consecrating today), through which we hear the voice of Christ calling us.

Bells ring out especially when Christ wants to tell us something important: they ring out on the great feasts of the Church, and they ring out every Sunday, announcing the day of the Lord.

Bells are also rung on the most important occasions in human life and mark these events in the life of each Christian; for example, they toll during our last earthly journey, to mark our passage to new, eternal life and to signify that death is in fact our birth to the Lord for all eternity.

Their sound is bound up with the wonderful mystery of the history of the Church, the history of the people of God. As we have just heard in the course of their consecration, bells still ring out in moments of great danger for the community, rather as if in the face of this danger they wanted to use their voice to express the prayer of the troubled human heart and the community which is struck by fear. They also ring in times of natural disaster when people in their fear turn to God in dumb silence.

The role of bells in the age-old tradition of the Church is very beautiful, and I am happy that you in the parish of Myślenice are today becoming a part of this long tradition. Under the leadership of your pastor you have obtained these new bells for your church, and your commitment to this cause was undoubtedly the fruit of your outstanding devotion to Our Lady of Myślenice, who was crowned here eight years ago as a sign of the special devotion of the people of God in this area. The bells are dedicated to her, and they must therefore speak to you of her presence and goodwill and must above all call you to her shrine to offer her your veneration. Together with her, they must pray for you and, together with you, turn to him.

My dear brothers and sisters of Myślenice, I want to express to you and your clergy my joy that you chose this fourth Sunday of Advent for the solemn blessing of these bells for your parish. And I want to express my hope that in this place that has been chosen by Mary as a shrine of her love and devotion these bells may carry out the mission I have just described to you. I hope that these bells— and, through them, you too, inasmuch as they are the expression of your faith and hopes—may fulfill their Advent mission as the voice crying in the wilderness. May they, expressing the spirit of Advent, be the voice of God as he draws near—that God for whom humanity is waiting and whom we sometimes forget even though he is the goal of our whole lives.

My wishes for these bells and for you all is that you may carry out this mission well. May they be eloquent in telling everybody that God is drawing near and in proclaiming his presence, holiness, mercy, and grace. May they be his forerunners, like John in the wilderness, and may they reach even those corners that nobody can reach, where people are alone and forget God. May their voice be accompanied by the grace of God himself, the grace of conversion and repentance, but also the grace of trust, joy and consolation, because this is how the grace they announce comes to us.

We dedicate these bells to the Mother of God, Our Lady of Myślenice, so that these signs of God's presence, which have been blessed today, may provide her with a convincing voice for our generation and for the generations to come, for the glory of God and the salvation of souls.

18 December 1977

7

❧

Christmas Eve

My dear ones, our gathering today has special significance in that it reminds us of those first meetings described in the earliest documents of the Church and of Christian history. We read about them in the Acts of the Apostles and even in the Gospels. These meetings were mainly eucharistic gatherings, just as today the first part of this meeting was also a eucharistic gathering. We broke and shared the bread of eternal life, and under the species of bread we received Christ, the eternal Word, the Son of the heavenly Father. However, we should never forget that those early Christian gatherings also had a family character, which is why they were called "fraternal love feasts" (*agapes*). Polish Christmas tradition is based on this aspect, which is expressed in the Christmas Eve supper at which the head of the family breaks and shares bread which is shaped like the host that is transformed into the body of Christ in the sacrament of the Eucharist. When Poles share in this blessed bread, they are carrying on the tradition which the early Christians called "the table of love."

My dear ones, in a few moments I shall bless all of you who are sharing in this fraternal love feast, especially the university students who have gathered in such numbers on this occasion. However, before this blessing I want to express my best wishes to you.

These wishes are prompted by the great divine mystery of Christmas, in which the Word became flesh. You have done well in preparing yourselves for Christmas here in this parish with your priests because only by turning our thoughts to God at this time can we understand the true value of each individual person without exception, beginning with ourselves. There is no other yardstick for human value, greatness, and dignity. Therein lies the mystery of Christmas. If we are able to read the depths of our souls and participate with our deepest sentiments, then on this Christmas Eve, in the light of the Christmas mystery each person truly takes on his own special value, illuminated by the light of the incarnate God, the God who became Man.

On Christmas Eve our thoughts go out to every person, seeking to reach them all, the disenfranchised, the abandoned, the persecuted, and even those who have brought such a condition on themselves. Christmas Eve has always meant the discovery of the true dimension of each and every person, of each and every one of our neighbors. The Holy Child reveals to us the sanctity of the human person.

Our wishes must therefore go out especially to the human person, to our neighbor as an individual. In our world, which is so marked by strong social bonds and increasing socialization, the human person is more and more often becoming part of an anonymous mass. This human anonymity must be illuminated by the mystery of the incarnate Word, by the God who became man, in order for the present moment to be seen in its full significance. These are my first wishes.

My second wish is also inspired by the Christmas mystery. The Son of God, the Son of the Father, is born. He reveals the interior life of God who is three and one. The Son of God becomes man as the Son of Mary. He becomes part of the human family and thus enables us all to share in his divine sonship. He is the brother of all, and through him the new human family comes into being. In no other way could people have been united or universal brotherhood brought about, since this is possible only through the support of the one Father, who is Father without any distinction between language, culture, or race or between poor or rich or between social, economic, or political class or system. One single Father and one single family.

Christmas is seen as a family festival, and today's gathering is imbued with this spirit. The bread that you receive here and that you will take back home is for the family: for your families, parents, children, brothers, sisters, relatives, and friends, in fact everybody who is gathered together with you in your home. It is for those families who are experiencing some crisis or are in some type of difficulty; for divided families; for families where the father or mother is missing and where the remaining parent must assume sole responsibility for the children. Christmas is a great night for all of them, a light that speaks to us of God the Father who wants to see people create a harmonious family community.

These thoughts are meant especially for the families to whom you owe your lives and to whom you return during this holiday period. However, it has a wider meaning, for you have grown up and are moving into the future, in which, in accordance with the laws of life, you will soon create families of your own. In the perspective of Christmas, what else could we wish you but that you should form strong families and be deeply united in that love which binds two people together indissolubly for the whole of life? I hope that you will be able to give love a truly human and divine dimension, thus fulfilling its highest potential. Love, marriage, and the family are the most fundamentally important elements in the life of human society and in that of any country.

While sharing this bread with you on this holy eve, I give you my wishes for the formation of real, healthy families. With this end in view, do not grudge your time, do not spare your prayer and your attention, and do not shirk any responsibilities or sacrifices. Marriage is a very great state of life, and I therefore hope that you will not waste it.

I have prayed with you around the altar tonight for these intentions. We have of course prayed for your studies and examinations and for your professional careers, but, my dear ones, the vocation to marriage and the family is the most crucial one. Like the priestly vocation, it is strictly personal in that one finds one's own self and one's true value as a person in it. The greatness of the family lies in its primary orientation towards the person, and this is why whoever marries and forms a family must be mature. I wish that maturity for all of you.

I also wish that you may overflow with humanity, that special and greatest of human gifts that is more important than intellectual ability, learning, art, or skill. I wish that you may have this treasure and that it may grow within you and spread out to others.

You are gathered here together representing our university city, and I imagine you living in its buildings, in those beautifully illuminated rooms I have passed by so many times and thought of you living in them. I meet you when I come to the church of Nowa Wieś at the beginning of the year or before Advent or during Lent.

What more do I wish for you? I wish that you may spread the good that you have within you throughout your homes and rooms.

Today in this world that is being more and more laicized, every Christian has a great mission. It is a world in which people are trying to impose atheism and move away from God without considering what they are losing or what priceless treasure is being buried, a world in which people are moving blindly, unaware of the cost, in the opposite direction from that of man's eternal destiny. Each Christian, with his heritage of faith, grace, hope, love, and vocation, must spread this treasure.

The windows of the university complex and the nearby streets are lit up. May your hearts and your young personalities shine forth in the same way, radiating this light. We must strive to make the atmosphere of these buildings both Christian and human. You have a great mission—and I am not afraid to use this word.

My dear ones, I wish you full human maturity. May you be true, conscious Christians, leaven in the midst of all those who live with you, so that they do not give up in advance or suffer frustration, because you are with them, you who break bread with me and have shared the body of Christ with me.

My dear ones, accept these wishes. Accept the truth they bring you—a Polish truth, rich in our Christmas tradition and deeply Christian.

Now I want to bless this special bread and each of you who hold it in your hands. Break it and share it with one another and with me and your priests and with your families at home. In this way we give new life to the ancient Polish vigil tradition in which at supper-time the father took the bread and blessed it and his family. In my position as father and priest, I bless this bread, and you and all those with whom you will share it. Go out and proclaim the good news of Christmas.

24 December 1973

* * *

I consider it a special grace both for you teachers and for us clergy to be gathered together here today. As we know, the Christmas season is marked by many such gatherings, beginning with the Christmas Eve supper in which the whole family joins.

Christmas Eve supper is a family affair that we spend with our loved ones, happy and sad alike, depending on the individual circumstances of each. It has a deeply religious meaning as a human reflection of the meeting between man and God which should take place on Christmas Eve.

We try to stretch the vigil spirit out as much as possible in order to gather together with different groups. Today's meeting with teachers, representatitves of the great teaching vocation, is especially welcome to us and is most precious and full of meaning. Indeed, you represent a field very close to our heart and of vital importance for the Church and for the life of our people, that is, the field of education.

Schooling does of course mean instruction. However, it would be a mistake to try and instruct people without educating them. It would be a mistake to form their intellect and their ideas, methods, principles, and concepts while ignoring their interior life. The humanistic tradition, and especially the Christian one, insists that the person is seen as an integral whole. Everything in him that is fruitful and brings intellectual fulfillment must also provide formation for his heart, will, and character; in other words, it must form the whole human person. The school is thus a place of education, and in this sense it is the extension and main support of the educational work of the family. This is the teaching of the Church as regards the school and the role it should fulfill.

The school must carry out the educational role entrusted to it by the family and must help the family by educating its children in areas beyond the capacity of the family itself. This task is vital for the life of our families and of our whole nation. The Church has a fundamental concern in this task since it plays a part in the educational process from its own particular perspective. The Church is aware of its position as the community of God's children who have become such through baptism.

Thus, in a society in which most people have been baptized, the Church must necessarily make its own particular contribution to education. If all those who go to school and who will make up the society of the future have become children of God through baptism, the Church naturally has a role to play in the educational process. In practical terms there must be active cooperation between Church and school.

This cooperation has now been abolished from the administrative or official veiwpoint, and we are all well aware that you are teachers in a state or lay school. However, the administrative abolition of such cooperation is one thing, and the live reality quite another. Any school that lives among people cannot avoid being the people's school and cannot avoid being at their service. And since our population is made up of baptized men and women, it is wrong to abolish cooperation between Church and school. Such a rupture would be an artificial and unfair imposition. This explains why, despite everything, cooperation between school and Church continues, not in any official or formal way, but in practical terms.

As clergy we are aware of this and feel its effects every day. This is particularly true as regards religious instruction, since, in general, catechism classes that take place outside the school are tolerated by the school and even looked on with a certain amount of goodwill. Schools try to facilitate catechism classes because there is a natural bond between school and people and thus between school and Church.

This bond has a variety of positive effects, and, although it may not be possible to list all of these, one of them is undoubtedly your presence here today. If I dared invite you (as I do in different places throughout the archdiocese) and if this invitation has been unanimously and wholeheartedly accepted, this means there is real cooperation between school staff and Church.

This cooperation springs from the fact that you are baptized, believing Christians, whose identity can never be artificially suppressed by anybody. Nobody can stop you from meeting with your bishop in his Krakow cathedral or offices or during a pastoral visit, for this is a right which springs from the fact that you are part of the community of the Church.

I am most grateful to you for your presence and am very happy with this whole meeting. In a few minutes I want to express my sincere good wishes to each one of you by sharing our special Christmas bread with you.

I hope that in your vocation as teachers and educators you may find every good thing for yourselves and for others and that in the school you may above all find personal fulfillment since you have chosen this particular way of life. We always find our own selves when we give something of ourselves to others, and you give everybody your teaching, your experience, and your work. I therefore hope that you will above all find your own selves in this way. I also hope that you may similarly discover others, that is, those whom you teach and educate. May your efforts meet with success and may your pupils listen to you without getting on your nerves! May everything you do in your work as teachers bear fruit day by day and week by week.

Moreover, I hope that carrying out your task and fulfilling your vocation, which is so important in the life of the nation and of the Church, may provide the means for saving your own souls (for this is in fact our main purpose in life) and also the means for helping others to save themselves, especially those to whom you teach the way of truth, goodness, and love. Your task is not that of proclaiming the gospel in explicit terms but rather that of proclaiming it by teaching the truth (be it the truth of literature, history, physics, chemistry, geography, or natural history) since the ways of the gospel and the ways of truth run parallel with one another. I therefore hope that you can show the way of salvation to those to whom you teach the truth and whom you educate in the truth.

I hope that in your school you and your students may be happy together and that you have a good relationship with them. Since most of your are married and have children, I also hope that your families, which are the preeminent school, may be better than those in which you work and that everything goes well within them.

After exchanging our greetings and good wishes, we shall sing some Christmas carols. I am sure that all Krakow will hear us then!

22 January 1978

8

❧

Midnight Mass

On this holy night together with the whole Church, we render our homage to the Son of God who is born in Bethlehem. Together with the whole Church, we welcome him with joy, singing: "Christ our Savior is born for us!"

The Son of God, who is coeternal with the Father, became man. As a citizen of the earth, his birth was registered right at the beginning of his life. In the history of the earth, Jesus Christ, the Son of God, received his citizenship as the Son of Mary, wife of Joseph. The gospel reading for today's liturgy reminds us of this.

Today, in an age when God is denied a place on earth, it should not be forgotten that he was listed among its inhabitants and assumed the nationality that would for the centuries to come be linked to the name of Jesus Christ.

He was born in the modest village of Bethlehem. Mary, wife of Joseph, had looked for a room in some inn where she could give birth, but in vain. God would be born in a nearby cave which was used as a stable, so that the Son of God would assume his human citizenship in a stable!

In the present age, in which God is denied citizenship among the inhabitants of our land and is refused a proper place in which to be born, we prepare a shed, a stable, a shelter in which he can come into the world, and when we gather together here we feel stronger because it seems to be the most similar place to where he was born.[1]

---

[1]Cardinal Wojtyla was celebrating this midnight Mass in the open air in the parish

Here we cradle our hopes: if God chose to be born in a stable and to assume his earthly citizenship there, then his birth among us under the open sky is the extension and authentic reenactment of that first birth.

This is how we twentieth-century Christians welcome Jesus Christ, the Son of God. This is how you, my dear brothers and sisters of this parish in the Krzeslawice hills, and I, Archbishop of Krakow, welcome him. I do not welcome him in the cathedral, but here with you in the authentic place of his birth, which throbs with the hope that he may be born for the future, for our future life, for the generations to come, for the next millenium. This is because it is here that we find that living faith, looked for in vain in the houses of Bethlehem but given him by shepherds in a stable.

In a few moments I shall take into my hands bread that will be very similar to the bread you broke and divided among you at your Christmas Eve supper. This bread and the wine that I shall take from your hands will be transformed, through the power of the words of consecration, into the Body and Blood of the Son of God. May he be born again at midnight from our bread and wine; from our love, faith, and community; from the good wishes we exchange; from our aspirations; and from the undeniably just request finally to be permitted to build a house for God here.

It is from all of this, under the form of bread and wine, that Jesus Christ will be born. We shall welcome him, as always, with faith and veneration, with hymns on our lips and with love in our hearts. We shall welcome him into our souls in order to live the life that he brings us. Even though he was born in a poor cave, he did not come empty-handed. He brought us, as he always will, the greatest gift of all—that of sharing his divinity, his condition as Son of God, with us. He makes us children of God, raising us up above ourselves and filling us with the gifts that God alone can give us.

All this will take place, my dear brothers and sisters, my dear

---

of Nowa Huta. This was also the case with the following two homilies in this book. He supported the inhabitants of this huge industrial suburb in their struggle to obtain a church. Eventually this hope was fulfilled, and as pope he visited the church, which had in large part been built by the workers themselves.

brother priests, through the offering of the bread which, as I have said, is so similar to the Christmas bread that you have broken and shared with one another in your homes. Here too we shall break and share bread, thus testifying to our faith in God's goodness and in the reality of his nearness and presence. May this faith pervade our whole life, both private, family and social, in this great modern industrialized Nowa Huta area of Krakow.

I join my best wishes, my dear brothers and sisters, to those you have already exchanged with one another and to the much greater one of the whole community that you may at last have a house in which Christ can be born. May he who has for centuries been listed and registered in this country be recognized as a citizen who, like others, has the right to a home.

24 December 1976

*   *   *

The Virgin who was about to give birth to her Son certainly deserved to have a roof over her head and a room in which to give birth. We cannot but feel that she should have had this; we feel that it is a basic human right, or a sort of law of nature, for a woman in childbirth to have a shelter. But no roof was found for her. There was no room for you when you came into the world. The only place to be found was a stable in a cave just outside the town of Bethlehem.

When we gather together in this place, we see again the Bethlehem cave in which the Son of God came into the world and was born of the Virgin Mary. When we come here to the Son of God, the newborn Christ, we find a remarkable similarity between this place and the Bethlehem shelter. Here too, for many years there has been no place for you, no roof under which to shelter you. But all of us, and with us Poland and the whole world, felt that a place must be found because people have the right to a roof when the desire to meet with God is born in their souls. This was the opinion of everybody in Poland, in Krakow, and in Nowa Huta.

I am speaking here in the perspective of two factors: first, that of the years I have lived here, and, secondly, that of recently having visited our fellow Poles across the Atlantic, where people know about your parish and feel it is of common interest to them too. This common interest has a special meaning. Today God who is born in human souls, just as he was born in Bethlehem long ago, should have a roof and a home. This is a human right and a law of nature. Other man-made laws must be subordinated to human rights and natural laws. It was an offense to God when no house, and not even a proper shelter, was found for him in Bethlehem, so that he had to be born in a stable in a cave.

The situation here is very eloquent; it is a moving symbol for us—and also for others as well. This is why we come each year to the place where this parallel is so clear, in order to greet Christ as he comes at midnight on Christmas Eve, to kneel before him in this particular spot which reminds us so strongly of that first Christmas despite the centuries which have passed.

As is the case each year, you have come here straight from your homes or your work in order to share the host in the great family of the parish. I am most sincerely grateful to you for the wishes that I have received from many quarters, and I should like to express my thanks to the clergy, religious sisters, and other members of the parish.

In turn I want to give you my best wishes and to call down the divine blessing on you, on each home, and on all those (whom I especially respect and admire) who perform heavy labor, on the sick, on the disenfranchised and disinherited, on parents, children, and young people—indeed, on the whole parish. This is how I want to return your good wishes to me.

Then, my dear brothers and sisters, let us in turn extend them to others from this Nowa Huta crib and eucharistic altar. My mind turns to all our fellow Poles across the ocean in Canada and the United States who have done so much for us. Let us try to wipe out the thousands of miles between us and them and invite them to this eucharistic table to share the host with us.

Let me also invite here today all the dioceses and parishes of Poland. And, since I have recently taken part in the synod of bishops in Rome, let me invite here the bishops or "shepherds" of all the different countries, continents and races in the world. In this night, we have but one heart, one faith, and one sentiment. One single heart beats in us for the God who is born and whose birth we celebrate each year, so that we too, through him, may become children of God.

This, my dear ones, is the great and universal community of all Christians, of the whole Church, of all of us who on this night live once again the birth of God into this world. We break and share bread, exchanging the same wishes as those expressed by the angels that night in Bethlehem: "Glory to God in the highest, and peace on earth to men of goodwill."

Tonight we are all of us overwhelmed and dumbfounded in the face of the divine love which took on human flesh and entered into the human spirit. We compare our miserable human love with his immeasurable love, and we pray that love may grow within us, that it may never be extinguished despite any difficulties or obstacles, and that it may never dim but always grow stronger.

May it never dim or fail, particularly in our families, in our marriages, and in relations between children and parents and between old and young. May it never fail in this Christian country. May it grow ever stronger within our society and withstand every effort to undermine or destroy it.

These are our wishes as we gather at this eucharistic table on which in a few moments, as at every Mass, Christ will be born to become our bread and to nourish us. Let us say to him today: "Welcome! Come to us, be our nourishment, and teach us to love."

This is our prayer, my dear brothers and sisters, and this our cry on this Christmas night in the year of Our Lord 1969. Together with the Holy Father and the whole Church, let us place it at the feet of Christ, who is about to be born of the Virgin Mother in this our Bethlehem.

24 December 1969

* * *

"In the silence of the night a voice rings out." In the silence of the night a voice echoed across the fields near Bethlehem, linking the glory of God in heaven with the peace of men on earth. The same voice later spread out from the countryside around Bethlehem to more and more places throughout the world, and today it echoes in the silence of Christmas night in every continent of the world.

The same voice has rung out for over a thousand years in Poland, here in Krakow, and in our other historical churches. And in a special way this Christmas voice, the voice of the midnight Mass, rings out in this place to which Christians come, like the Bethlehem shepherds long ago, to gather around the crib. They come to this place that so clearly reminds us of the shelter in which God came into the world because he could not find a proper roof.

"In the silence of the night a voice rings out, 'Rise up, shepherds, God is being born.' " And then it adds, "Run with all speed to Bethlehem."

Bethlehem was a small town in Palestine that became famous as the birthplace of Our Lord Jesus Christ, and the name means "house of bread." Today, and especially tonight, the whole of our country is transformed into one great "house of bread." In the course of supper in many homes, our fellow Poles have broken bread and shared it with one another. We too have done this, exchanging our good wishes, not only in the homes of our parish but also here before the celebration of midnight Mass. I should like to thank you and to offer you my warmest good wishes in return.

My wishes are for your own deepest desires, and concern the worries, problems, noble aspirations, and preoccupations of all who live here. They are also specifically concerned with this place and the wholehearted wish that a house of bread, or Bethlehem, may be built here among these huge modern structures—a house to which people can come to feed on the bread which is the Body of Christ and gives eternal life, a real house of bread for those who live in this area and not simply a wretched roofless spot. You and I are all doing everything we can and making every possible effort to bring this about. What have we achieved so far? We have not received any official permission. However, as we were assured by the regional authorities in Krakow at their last meeting with your bishop, there is widespread agreement that a church will be built in this neighborhood.

We can see this as a reward for our perseverance. However, it is only a beginning, and we shall bring this matter up again, pointing out that the local authorities have given their word in this regard. We shall thus try to make sure that this promise is kept, so that all of us who live in this area can have our own house of bread where Christ can be born in a properly protected place.

These are my wishes for the whole parish and community, your clergy, religious sisters, young people, children, parents, the sick—indeed, all of you.

The same Christmas carol that sings of the angel's call to the shepherds to go to Bethlehem continues: "They went and found the Child lying in the manger." With these words in mind I want to express an even deeper wish than those of a few moments ago. I hope that all those who live in the area around this pastoral center dedicated to Blessed Queen Hedwig* may come and find Christ; and this wish applies to every single person, not just to those who are here and have thus already found Christ but also to those who for various reasons are not here with us—because they do not believe they can find him or because they have lost him or because they are afraid. The reason makes no difference. I wish that all of them may find Christ, because he is the Savior of the world.

These are the wishes I want to offer you, my dear brothers and sisters, at this Christmas Eucharist. I would ask you to welcome them into your hearts, take them back home with you, and live in harmony with them. In the same way, I too shall find new life in the wishes you have offered me today in the name of your community.

May this Christmas that we are celebrating increase the birth and presence of God in your souls and in all souls, in the soul of the whole nation, which prays to the infant Jesus: "Raise your little hand, O Holy Child, and bless our beloved homeland."

---

*Blessed Hedwig (1374-1399) was crowned queen of Poland at the age of ten and died in childbirth at the age of twenty-five. The cause for her canonization is at present under consideration.

This is our prayer on Christmas Eve at the close of the Holy Year of 1975 and at the beginning of the last quarter century of the second millenium after Christ. We pray to him, as our ancestors have prayed to him for many centuries: "Raise your little hand, O Holy Child, and bless our beloved homeland."

24 December 1975

9

❧

Christmas Day

In the stately metropolitan Cathedral of Wawel we are today concelebrating Mass after the close of the Second Vatican Council. On the feast of Christmas, we are concelebrating at the altar of Saint Stanislaus, bishop and martyr, patron saint of Krakow, of our archdiocese, and of the whole of Poland*; we bishops from this archdiocese who took part in the Second Vatican Council are celebrating this Holy Mass together. When we celebrate the Eucharist together we are trying to express the deep truth of the priesthood of Jesus Christ. As we know, when a priest celebrates Mass alone, he represents Jesus Christ, as his living, intelligent, and conscious instrument, so that in the priest we see Christ himself. When many of us celebrate—or concelebrate—Mass together, the number of celebrants makes it easier for us to understand that there is in fact only one priest who celebrates the eternal sacrifice and that this priest is Jesus Christ. Every priest and bishop who has received the sacrament of orders bows down before the deepest and only fullness of the priesthood that belongs to Jesus Christ himself.

Today we are celebrating the Eucharist in thanksgiving to God, one in the Holy Trinity, for the Council, and we want to bow down before the fullness of the one priesthood of Christ. We gaze on him with faith and love in the Bethlehem crib, and with the same faith

*Saint Stanislaus (1030-1079) was bishop of Krakow and was killed by King Boleslaus II while celebrating the Eucharist. He was canonized in 1253 and is the patron saint of Poland.

and love we recognize that he is present sacramentally, but just as effectively and just as full of grace, here in the Holy Mass.

Kneeling before the crib, we see the infant Jesus, the Son of God, the incarnate Word, lying on the straw, and we see his first moment on earth at the very beginning of his mission. He came and lived among us, and he wants to stay with us. And this is how the Second Vatican Council, reflecting on Jesus in the crib in Bethlehem, rediscovered more deeply and fully its true task. The Church has rediscovered itself and stated that its meaning comes from the mystery of the Incarnation, the mystery of the Father who sends his Son, and the mystery of the Holy Spirit, who is sent by the Father and the Son.

The Church is a true, homogeneous extension of the divine missions—or "sendings"—of the Son and the Holy Spirit, and herein lies its deepest essence. The mission of the Son and the Holy Spirit, which took place within time, is still continuing through people who receive the Son and who, through the interior action of grace, themselves become the mystical body of Christ and the people of God.

These truths may seem very simple, but they had to wait to be rediscovered, formulated, and expressed. In the Second Vatican Council, the Church has thus formulated and described its own supernatural, holy essence.

However, the work of the Church does not end with these definitions. The Son of God, whom we see in the manger today, was sent into the world, for the world. He entered into the world and is a living part of the human race; he belongs to humanity and remains with it. Similarly, the Church entered into the world, belongs to humanity, and remains closely bound to it. This is why it was not enough for the Second Vatican Council to produce definitions regarding the interior nature of the Church; it also had to express the attitude of the Church toward the world.

At this point I should like to tell you that I was fortunate enough to play a special role in the work of the part of the Council that dealt with what was known as *Schema 13*, which later became known as the Pastoral Constitution on the Church in the Modern World.* Ev-

---

Gaudium et spes, issued on 7 December 1965. The author was speaking on 25 December of the same year.

erything I am telling you now therefore comes from my own personal experience. I remember all the meetings of the commission held last winter and spring and then the meeting of the whole Council this fall.

When we considered the contemporary world, we noted two particularly pressing problems. The first concerns progress and development in the scientific and other fields. This progress must go hand in hand with the development of the interiority, humanity, and personality of the person, who was created in the image and likeness of God. This is the basic problem. However, in complete contrast to this we see signs of things that threaten man and that spring from this progress and development. The first and greatest threat is that of war with all the weapons of destruction that technical progress and our civilization have brought into being.

On this point the attitudes of the Council and of all humanity are in agreement. In a way the ideas expressed by the Council developed out of the attitudes of John XXIII. I remember the moment in 1962 when he announced the Council and how at the very beginning of its work there was a strong risk of war. Thanks to the pope (and everybody recognizes this) the threat was averted. John XXIII then devoted the rest of his days to writing the encyclical *Pacem in terris.*

The ideas and attitudes of the pope who convened the Council found their echo in his successor Paul VI. Their personalities may be different, but their orientation is the same. I came to understand this personally, since I was fortunate enough to observe both pontiffs closely during the Council. Pope Paul VI, and with him the Council, developed the ideas of his predecessor, paying special attention to the threats hanging over humanity today (particularly the risk of war, which has potential flashpoints in a wide variety of problems and areas of conflict) and also studying theories of human development. In this way they produced a just formula and valid principle for working towards the restoration of harmony in the problems afflicting humanity today. This formula is known as *dialogue.*

You may ask about the precise meaning of the word *dialogue,* which is a word we know and frequently use and which may appear to be more or less equivalent to the word *conversation*. When two people talk together, we say that a dialogue is taking place; whereas when only one person speaks, we say that it is a monologue. However, this explanation is too superficial, since dialogue is much more than a simple conversation or an exchange of words or ideas. Dialogue is a human attitude deriving from the fact that man is a person called to live with others in society. Dialogue entails not only the capacity to speak but also the capacity to listen, the capacity to speak in such a way that the other can understand, and the capacity to listen in such a way as to understand the other. Dialogue is a human attitude and is an attribute of the person endowed with a social sense. Such an attitude is also deeply Christian because it can be used as an effective means of eliminating hatred and human conflict. Dialogue and conflict are contradictory terms.

Thus the Church today, through its pontiffs and through the Council, is telling people in every part of the world never to base human relations on conflict, but on dialogue instead.

Dialogue is a fundamental expression in today's Church, and we see its value in daily life. We know that between two people, for example husband and wife, dialogue can be used to resolve problems happily. If each of us insisted on his own monologue, we would be running the risk of conflict because monologue often does lead to conflict. If I think in my own way and say what I want, without the slightest thought as to whether the other hears and understands me because I do not hear and understand him either, we shall inevitably clash. This happens on every level of human life.

While I might even dare say that in the past humanity could permit itself the indulgence of war, this is no longer true today, since we have such immense means of destruction at our disposal.

Our reflections on the world and on the mission of the Church make it ever clearer what dialogue fundamentally is. The Church and the Council draw this conclusion not only from the contemporary situation of mankind and society but first and foremost from the crib and the cross—as Paul VI wrote in his first encyclical, which dates from 1964, and which begins with the words *Ecclesiam*

Suam. Revelation, redemption, and then faith, prayer, and the whole Christian life, are the substance of God's dialogue with man and man's with God. Through this dialogue, which the eternal Father carries on with humanity through his Son and the Holy Spirit, he teaches us how to find the means of resolving difficult human problems. This is what the Council tried to discern and find in the manger, in revelation, and on Calvary, in order to be able to proclaim it to men and women today.

I now want to pass on to you one of the basic concepts and principles of the Church which has been given fresh emphasis in the course of the Council. The Church has not simply formulated ideas and proclaimed principles but actively seeks to open dialogue and set an example in resolving difficult or controversial problems. Thus the Church is entering into dialogue—or is at least trying to do so—with followers of other religions and also with non-believers and atheists.

Although these are of course the first steps, they have been deeply considered and are dictated by concern for the good of mankind and humanity as a whole and not only for the good of the Church. When the Church bows before the manger and kneels before the cross, it is aware that all humanity has been redeemed and that the mission of the Son and the Holy Spirit is directed to all humanity and hence that the same applies to its own mission. Today I am trying to pass on to you this enriched concept of the Church.

We are concelebrating our Christmas Mass at the tomb of Saint Stanislaus, bishop and martyr. You may find this linking of cradle and tomb rather strange, but we are here because this tomb saw the birth of a life. The birth of the Church in our country has its place within the framework of God's unceasing activity; and this tomb is the cradle of its birth. I am not saying that it marks the absolute beginning, although to a significant extent this is in fact so. So here we are at the cradle of Poland's faith, around the crib that is the symbol of the Nativity.

At the beginning of October 1962 when I left to take part in the Council as vicar of the Archdiocesan Chapter of Krakow, this is the spot from which I took my leave and on which you bade me farewell. When I said then that I was leaving the tomb of Saint Stanislaus in order to go to the tomb of Saint Peter, I emphasized this because these two places are closely linked. For us the tomb of Saint Stanislaus at Wawel and the tomb of Saint Peter in Rome are closely connected.

When I left from here, I took with me, as it were, the whole of the Krakow church and indeed the whole of the Polish church, inasmuch as throughout the centuries Saint Stanislaus, bishop and martyr, has been seen as patron and protector of the Polish church. I took our Polish church to the universal Church of Christ, as it revealed and expressed itself in the Council. Our church of Saint Stanislaus was present there in the universality, unity, and great communion of all the churches of the world. Through myself and the other Polish bishops, our church took part in the renewal of the Church. Thus the ancient, thousand-year-old church of Krakow, the Polish church, was reaffirmed in the universality of the Church of Christ. It was strengthened in its meeting with all the churches and dioceses of the whole world—those of Europe, the Americas, Africa, Asia, and Oceania. Our church was reaffirmed and strengthened every day for many months in its constant contact and daily communion with bishops from every part of the world. Communion means a bond or unity, and *communio episcoporum, communio ecclesiarum* (communion of bishops, communion of churches) has been a great grace for our Polish church.

At the Council there were bishops of dioceses which are centuries older (and even a thousand years older) than ours, and there were others from churches which are much younger than ours, so that we lie between one extreme and the other because in Poland Christianity began more or less in the middle of the history of the Church to date, at the end of the first millenium and the beginning of the second.

In the course of the Council the dialogue opened among more than two thousand bishops formed the basis for the renewal of the Church, and in our experience and in our dialogue within the Church we looked for bases for a renewal of all humanity.

This is the situation now that we are approaching the beginning of the second millenium since the baptism of Poland. The Christmas we are now celebrating is the last one of the first millenium.

While experiencing the unbroken unity of bishops during the Council, we felt the wish to speak to them about our thousand years and our great Christian jubilee in the spirit of community that united us to them and all humanity. If only you knew how great the community of the Church is that unites us to the whole Christian world—not only to those in European countries but also to those much farther afield!

We also though of our closest neighbors from a geographical viewpoint who have been separated from us by history (but also united with us, inasmuch as divisions also unify). We gave a great deal of hard thought to how to speak of our thousand years with the bishops and other Catholics of Germany, who is our westerly neighbor. Some people would maybe have wanted to express our hatred to them. But, my dear ones, would this have been possible after a thousand years of Christianity in Poland and after a thousand Christmases celebrated in this land? There may of course be people who would like to have told them that they have been and continue to be our enemies. But I ask you how we Polish bishops could have said this on the threshold of the celebration of a thousand years since our baptism.

Instead, we started by saying: "Our brothers in Christ, bishops of Germany, for centuries and especially more recently your country has done terrible things to us." We could say that in a certain way we have in fact confessed for them the terrible things that the German people have done to us. We have confessed it in its unvarnished truth, including Auschwitz and the six million victims of the last war, without hiding or glossing anything over. We have anticipated their confession. When we take a look at the two letters (ours to the German bishops and theirs to us) and read them carefully without omitting anything, we can see how, through our confession, they have confessed.*

---

*This exchange between the Polish and German bishops had given rise to fierce discussion between the former and the Polish government, which is probably why Wojtyla gave this explanation here.

Briefly we told them that we forgave them and asked them to forgive us. We said that we forgave them inasmuch as they too, under the stimulus of our confession, had also made an open confession. We asked them to forgive us above all because in the solemn letter marking our millenial year we had said many unpleasant things, and when one says unpleasant things, one must then ask forgiveness, and then in the second place because we were aware than in any relationship between persons (especially one lasting for many years) there is always something to be forgiven on both sides.

And now, my dear ones, we have come back from the tomb of Saint Peter on the Vatican hill to the tomb of Saint Stanislaus on the Wawel hill, bringing with us the whole Council, the renewal of the Church, and the fundamental principle of dialogue.

Many years ago, the first conciliar father in Polish history, Bishop Vincent Kadlubek, left from this city to attend the Lateran Council and later returned to renew the church in this country. Similarly, we bishops are also returning in order to renew the Polish church in the context of the universal Church. You must help us in the task with which we are faced and for which we pray to God during today's Mass. Help us to renew our holy church of Saint Stanislaus. Let us all work together in this church to renew our people and, through our own renewal, contribute to the renewal of the whole of humanity. May my words as bishop kindle your hearts for this renewal, which we place on the tomb of Saint Stanislaus.

My dear brother priests and religious sisters, we want to arouse a great desire for renewal in you, and this concelebration should mark the beginning. With this same end in view, the Holy Father has asked that at the end of the Council, from 1 January to Pentecost, a special jubilee should be celebrated throughout the Church with the cathedral as its center in each diocese. We must therefore gather together more frequently in this Cathedral of Saint Stanislaus in Wawel and pray more intensely with special faith and sentiments of mutual forgiveness in our hearts. We shall gather together here, coming in pilgrimage to this holy place, which is the church of the living God in our land.

Reverend brothers of the cathedral chapter, I want to place this postconciliar jubilee under your special care and protection. It must mark the beginning of the renewal of our lives in Christ and in his Church.

As your bishop I should like to express my wish that all of you, my beloved fellow citizens of Krakow, who have gathered here to relive together the mystery of the birth of Our Lord Jesus, the mystery of the Incarnation, may live in the truth. The Son of God is the Word, and the Word is the Truth. I wish that you may live in Christ, in the Truth and in the Love which come from God.

25 December 1965

* * *

On this great feast of Christmas, together with your most excellent bishop and the cathedral chapter as guardians and ministers of this holy shrine of our nation and church, I offer my wholehearted greetings and best wishes to you who have come to this majestic Wawel Cathedral. I would also link my greetings to those of the group from the seminary who are always of such assistance to us in the cathedral. Our greetings go out to all of you here present, especially the citizens of Krakow, and not only of the old city but also of the new one of Nowa Huta.

In a special way I should like to welcome the members of the parish of Saint Casimir who have been invited to share in today's celebrations. My dear ones, you have come here with your parish clergy in order to show the bond that unites your parish and church with the bishop and cathedral that is the mother of all the churches in the Archdiocese of Krakow. During Advent I made a pastoral visit to your parish and our meeting today in this cathedral, at the tombs of Saint Stanislaus and Blessed Queen Hedwig, sets the seal, so to speak, on that Advent meeting.

My dear brothers and sisters, today we are all filled with the Christmas joy which comes from the faith that God has been born into the world. However, our joy must expand and spread, so that each year it embraces new thoughts and events and brings them into the joy of Christmas, in order that the mystery of the Incarnation may grow fuller and fuller each year until the end of time. This is what today's liturgy teaches us.

While I am speaking to you, a great many of you will undoubtedly be thinking of that small group of men who are orbiting the moon*—a remarkable event in the history of science and human technology. For the first time man has left the earth, in the literal sense of the term, moving beyond the barrier of the atmosphere and gravity of our earth, and is now orbiting another celestial body. Throughout the world people are thinking of this event and of their representatives who are the first to perform such a feat, and they are wondering with a certain amount of fear and apprehension whether they will come back safely to earth.

Events like these and the thoughts they engender make us realize that human reality is also expressed in this type of feat.

Man is an entity who is constantly seeking and moving beyond the limits of previous accomplishments, so that human history is the history of culture and civilization, in which emphasis is always placed on the desire to transcend previous limits. This tendency derives from human nature, thought, and creative capacity and also from the will to dominate creation, which the Creator planted in the human soul. Thus, God told our earliest ancestors: "Fill the earth and subdue it" (Genesis 1:28).

In line with this, man always looks to the future, discovering new things and finding out more and more about the visible reality of the created world. He gains ever greater knowledge of the laws that govern this world and comes more and more fully to dominate and make use of nature. In this way he becomes more and more the lord of creation, in accordance with the plan of his Creator.

The truth about man, which has been illustrated for us particularly clearly this Christmas when men are for the first time orbiting the moon, is also oriented in a special way towards the mystery of Christmas, which we are reliving today.

God came into the world! What does this mean? It means, my dear brothers and sisters, that he came to meet the aspirations im-

---

*The manned lunar orbital mission of the U.S. space craft Apollo VIII lasted from 21 to 27 December 1968.

printed within man to move beyond himself, to obtain more, and to be always something more. God takes these aspirations into account and, becoming man, shows man the true purpose of the possibilities that are found not in creation or in the visible world but in God himself. Man can transcend himself not only through his progress within the world: he can transcend himself through becoming a son of God, as today's gospel tells us.

Man was created in the image and likeness of God and becomes as completely as possible like his Creator and Father if, within creation, he becomes a son of God. Here we have another aspect of humanity's movement beyond itself. This is an interior transcendence with the help of the Spirit, in which man in his spiritual essence moves beyond his own spirituality and his humanity and comes to share in divinity itself. The Christmas mystery proclaims this to us, especially through the readings for today's Mass: "To all who received him . . . he gave power to become children of God" (John 1:12). "He gave power." He gave power to dominate the earth, the created world, the whole cosmos. He gave us this power, and we in turn develop it; and this is what leads to human progress in the world.

However, he also gave us the power to become children of God. He showed us this power when he was born in a stable in Bethlehem. Now in 1968, a very long time later, when we see how we have developed this first, natural power, we must also reflect on the extent to which we have developed our second, supernatural power. To what extent have we become children of God? This is an important question because if there were too great an imbalance between the first and second types of human development, this would constitute a danger for the human race.

Thus, my dear brothers and sisters, when we gather around the crib, we must feel that we are God's children, so that we regain that interior equilibrium and maturity that come from God, who is born today in Bethlehem. I have invited you to Wawel Cathedral in order to revive this awareness in you and also because this cathedral is, so to speak, the great cradle of the Polish spirit. The whole building (the altar, before which the Polish kings were crowned; the tomb of

Saint Stanislaus, bishop and martyr and patron saint of Poland; and the tomb of Queen Hedwig, together with all the other monuments to our kings, military heroes, prophets, and bishops) is like a perennial crib for the unceasing birth of Christ in the history of the people of God in Poland. This is why each year at this Christmas daytime Mass we must gather in veneration around this Wawel crib, which is the cradle of our spiritual strength, which has come and always will come from God, just as the shepherds and the magi gathered around the manger in Bethlehem.

This year the divine Mother has revealed herself in a special way at the cradle of our archdiocese, and in a special way the Mother of God, Queen of Poland, Our Lady of Jasna Gora, has, through grace, given birth to Christ within our hearts.

Strengthened in the Spirit, we recall and give thanks for all these gifts. May our offering at this Bethlehem crib in Wawel be a new step towards the spiritual destiny of all of us gathered here and of the church of Krakow and the whole of our beloved country that we always remember as we sing: "Raise your little hand, O Holy Child, and bless our beloved homeland. In righteousness and soundness of life, may it base its strength on your strength, O fragile newborn Babe, on your strength!"

25 December 1968

* * *

Christmas Eve is now over, midnight has struck, and dawn has broken, and we have all been caught up in the Christmas mystery, first through our vigil gathering around the family dining table and then by flocking in great numbers to midnight Mass or the dawn celebration; and now, as midday approaches, we have come here to the solemn eucharistic liturgy in Wawel Cathedral. The constant theme is that of gathering around the mystery of Bethlehem, the crib, the Word made flesh who has come to dwell among us.

The shepherds who were watching over their flocks came to find the child who had been born at midnight in a cave outside the city, and at the manger they were joined by the chorus, which sang hymns to God's glory. Later the wise men also arrived. And following the example of these different groups, we too come at different times—evening, night, dawn, and morning—in order to relive this divine mystery that is also the greatest human event.

Like those who came first, we come to contemplate and to bow down and acknowledge God in the mystery of his Incarnation; and when we come, we find ourselves. Contemporary people in this last quarter of the twentieth century, whose human dignity has been ignored and infringed in so many ways, come to Christ's stable in Bethlehem to ask who they are and why they are in the world, bringing with them their existential anxiety. And when they come to Bethlehem, like each of us they find the reply in the manger on the straw: "I have given them power to become children of God." This small, weak infant, who was born and forced to stay outside the town in a stable, has given this power—and he still gives it to us who live in the twentieth century and whose human dignity and essence have been so compromised that we no longer really understand that we were made in the image and likeness of God. However, this truth alone gives meaning to our human existence, and only in this truth do we find the answer to the questions of who we are and why we are alive.

The Son of God became man in weakness, to help us to be fully human, giving us the power to become children of God.

Although it is true that we come to Bethlehem to bring gifts, it is in fact we who receive them. And, indeed, when we consider the gifts brought by people, whether poor shepherds or rich kings (and this includes all of us), we are mainly talking of things they have found or received.

There is a great deal of discussion of human rights today, with people trying to define them and lay down their principles, and we are right to see this as a constructive contribution of our century. However, it must also be said that in this same century the very concept of humanity has been challenged and undermined. We must therefore defend the rights of the human person.

The first defender of human rights lies in the manger on the hay. He defined and ordained this dignity when he, the Son of God and coexistent with the Father, became one of us—a man.

Many people from different parts of the world come to Bethlehem to find him. And today the Polish people have come to this cathedral. Sad to say, however, if we read the official press, we shall find no mention at all of Christmas as such. It is spoken of as if it were just an ordinary holiday with designs of evergreen branches and little candles in an effort to hide the true light it brings. Nor do we find on the newsstands any mention of the close link between this birth and the birth of our nation.

The mystery of Jesus, who was born in Bethlehem to the Virgin Mary, has for a thousand years shaped the soul of our people in their history, culture, and traditions. Our identity is bound up with the mystery of Christmas, and in every period of our nation's history, from medieval times down to the nineteenth century and even to our own days, we find indications of what is completely ignored in today's press, even during the Christmas season.

However, despite the attitude of the official press in this period, hymns of joy rise up from every quarter, not only during midnight Mass but also in every home, and beautifully decorated Christmas trees twinkle and shine throughout our country. All this is not simply folklore but bears witness to our identity as Poles and testifies to how, with him, our nation is reborn on this night each year, generation after generation. "This is a sacred night for us," as Wyspianski wrote.*

On this night the Polish people come to the Bethlehem crib, speaking of themselves and their history, their past and their mission, their victories and defeats and sufferings, and of their present condition. And as they speak they show who they are and who they want to be!

It is sometimes said that a new Poland must come into being. But Poland is a unique entity, and if this other, second one wants to remain Poland, it must be born from the first, since we can never deny or suppress our national and cultural heritage in any aspect.

*The Polish nationalist poet and playwright Stanislaus Wyspianski (1869-1907).

Thus the people of Poland as they exist today in 1976 come to the Bethlehem crib, bringing their special heritage with their past, present, and future to the One who is born in a stable. We have no intention of denying our own identity.

The proposals sometimes made regarding education and the teaching of history and literature tend to increase our fear of a weakening of our identity. With this fear in our hearts, we, who are the people of God in Poland, come to the Bethlehem cave. With this fear but also with a thousand-year-old hope, we come to him who became man and made himself a weak infant whom we find lying in the hay. We entrust the rights of our people to him, the rights of man as individual and society, respect for which constitutes the first precondition for peace on earth.

In Bethlehem, the heavenly spirits used human voices to express this truth in song: "Glory to God in the highest and peace on earth to men of goodwill." We bring all our problems and anxieties to the Bethlehem stable, and there we come to realize that peace can be obtained only if the rights of the individual and of the population as a whole are respected. It is therefore not enough to repeat these words; we must put them into practice and mold circumstances. These thoughts have brought us twentieth-century Poles to the Bethlehem stable for the various Christmas celebrations both yesterday and today.

I want to express my greetings and best wishes to all of those present here, to the members of the cathedral chapter, my brother priests, and the representatives of the parishes of Mistrzejowice, Azory, and Krowodrze (whose patron saint is Blessed Queen Hedwig). These wishes are the same as those the heavenly Father sent through his angels, when with human voices they proclaimed: "Glory to God in the highest and peace on earth to men of goodwill."

25 December 1976

10

❦

The Feast of Saint Stephen

Today your parish community is celebrating the feast of Saint
Stephen, the first martyr. This saint, who has been venerated
throughout the Church from apostolic times, is particularly hon-
ored in your parish, which chose him as its patron saint. Today the
Diocese of Krakow and I, as its bishop, are here to venerate him
with you.

We celebrate this solemn feast, my dear brothers and sisters, immediately after that of Christmas. In this way in accordance with
age-old tradition we link the joy of Christmas to the memory of
Saint Stephen, as if the blood shed by this martyr was a sort of necessary complement. Yesterday we commemorated the birth of our
Savior, the birth of him who came to give life by shedding his
blood, and today we have the witness of the blood of the martyred
Saint Stephen.

In that early community, Stephen belonged to the group of disciples and was outstanding for the strength of his active faith, which
was why he was made a deacon. His faith was lived out in love that
led him to serve all those in need, and we find descriptions of his
service in the Acts of the Apostles.

However, from the very beginning the Church has remembered
Stephen principally for the way he witnessed to his faith at every
possible opportunity. His witness was foremost one of deeds but
also of words. He expressed his faith in Jesus Christ in words, and it

was because of this that the crowd "ground their teeth against him" and "stopped their ears" and then stoned him to death (Acts 7:54-60).

Today when the whole Church is united in celebrating the feast of Saint Stephen, the first martyr, we should reflect on this question of bearing witness, which has always been an essential aspect of our faith. Faith does not merely mean the interior state of the human conscience, intellect, and convictions, nor does it refer simply to a certain echo in the heart. Faith is open confession or acknowledgment. Christ said this clearly: "Every one who acknowledges me before men, the Son of man also will acknowledge before the angels of God" (Luke 12:8).

Christ linked the confessions of the disciple and the master together, and in today's liturgy we find them together again. As Stephen fell beneath the shower of stones, he cried out: "I see the heavens opened, and the Son of man standing at the right hand of God" (Acts 7:56). "I shall acknowledge him before my Father." The confession or witness of the disciple Stephen bore that fruit which Christ promised to all those who acknowledge him before others. Christ acknowledged Stephen before his Father.

We are living in a very precise social context today, and it is important that we accept the truth of our faith without any hesitation or reserve. This must be expressed through religious confession and must not consist simply of some interior state about which other people know nothing. We must not be halfhearted about our convictions but must be clear and firm—even if this is sometimes inconvenient. Thus the question of religious confession and of bearing witness to Christ has great contemporary relevance.

However, we must not exaggerate this problem in our minds. Sometimes we do tend to place too much weight on such considerations as "What will they do to me, can they fire me, can they ruin my career?" before we have even undergone this test of Christian strength and openly confessed our religious faith. Such timorousness saps the strength of each of us and of our community as a whole, because the strength of the community of the Church depends on the faith of each of its members.

Of course an event like midnight Mass here at Krowodrze in the Krzeslawice hills gives us a feeling of strength. This strength must be found in each one of us. Christ spoke clearly about the personal confession of faith—"every one who acknowledges me before men"—and we must reflect deeply on these words. We should be careful that this strength is not lost in our society of believing Catholics, so that we none of us as individuals give an impression of uncertainty about our identity and beliefs.

My dear brothers and sisters, I have no intention of offending or insulting any particular person by speaking in this way. Heaven forbid! I am simply discussing a matter that is of perennial importance in the lives of both laity and clergy.

Our faith is our strength, and confessing it is the strength of our society; it is also the strength of each individual and manifests our human dignity not only to unbelievers but also to those who seek to harm us because of our faith. Our confession of faith and our identification of ourselves as Christians elicits respect and gives us a sense of dignity. Harmony between what we feel within ourselves and what we manifest outwardly is a great value and its absence constitutes a threat to human dignity. Indeed, harmony between word and action and between belief and confession of faith provides the measure of human dignity.

The things the Church admires about Saint Stephen are the witness he bore to Christ and his confession of faith. And bearing witness to Christ and professing one's faith should be a civil right, assured and guaranteed within society. This right should be formulated in such a way that freedom of religion does not refer only to freedom of conscience and faith but also to its outward expression on both the personal and communal levels.

The right of the believing Christian citizen to bear witness to Christ is present when there is freedom of the written or spoken word and consequently freedom to behave in accordance with this. This is a basic constitutional right in any democratic society in which the human person is respected. If the person is denied freedom of speech, so that his words are censored and made to conform to specific norms, then he is not being respected, and this system of life is no longer truly human either from a social or individual viewpoint.

I recently read something interesting about von Galen, who was bishop of Münster during the Hitler era and whose name is probably familiar to you. In this article a Pole recalled that during the occupation this bishop's sermons were passed from hand to hand in typewritten form since they could obviously not be printed and published. This means that in line with his sense of his ministry and the dictates of his conscience the bishop proclaimed the truth—a truth in clear opposition to the totalitarianism of the German government.

We should not be surprised at this. Christ's words elicited such a dramatic reaction that they crucified him. Saint Stephen's words elicited a similar reaction and they stoned him to death. We should not be surprised that this sort of thing happened in the early days.

However, in this more enlightened era, such actions are clearly incompatible with sensitivity to human rights and the rights of the citizen. Today people cannot behave like that—just as a bishop cannot be prevented from publishing his sermons, even in his diocesan newsletter. However, the state does censor what the Church says, including even the words of its head, sometimes going so far as to suppress texts dealing with moral matters.

We want to give our witness of faith, and we shall never stop giving it. This witness, which is simply the manifestation of the teachings of the Church, must have civil rights in the life of our society, which is overwhelmingly Catholic. Freedom of speech, whether written or spoken, is a fundamental human right and proof in any state and under any type of government that the person is respected. Let us refuse to accept that it exists only for those who hold other views; we must insist that it is neither suppressed nor restricted.

As you can see, my dear brothers and sisters, these matters touch closely on your call to bear witness. That German bishop to whom I have just referred (and who later became a cardinal in the same year as our unforgettable Archbishop Stefan Sapieha) bore his own testimony in this regard. Today we remember him with respect and without any prejudice about his German background. A bishop must bear witness, and the same applies to a priest or to any other Christian.

Any society or governmental system ruled according to the principles of justice, in which the person and his ideas are respected, also protects freedom of speech, whether written or spoken. In such a society each person can express his own religious faith publicly, whether as a community or as an individual, be he priest, bishop, seminarian, or layman.

I mention seminarians purposely because when they are drafted into the army they bear special witness to their faith throughout the period of their service, making every type of sacrifice in order to pray. The attitude of their superiors is always that it is all right for them to pray secretly but that nobody else must know about it. However, the seminarians always reply by pointing out that they are witnesses of Christ. They will soon be priests and they cannot hide the fact that they pray. And so they pray, despite all types of harassment, which I would prefer not to describe in detail.

For us Poles the problem of witness is becoming more and more serious in our social life and in our culture. As Christians we are never considered in the daily press. However, we are part of the Polish people and as such we have the right to read about ourselves and our life and about the truths and issues which concern us.

What can we say about the fact that the only Catholic sociocultural periodical (which is published here in Krakow) has for years been refused permission to increase its press run from forty-five thousand to fifty thousand copies? I am of course referring to *Tygodnik Powszechny*.* This is taking place in a country with thirty-four million inhabitants. I cannot say how many of these thirty-four million are Catholics, although we do know that the majority of them have been baptized. This, too, is a question of witness. We bear witness through prayer, words, and actions. We want to bear witness with our actions and through the press, television, and radio, and we want to feel that we are free to do so in the knowledge that there is a place for us believers in the mass media of our nation.

*The General Weekly. This nonpolitical publication was founded by Cardinal Sapieha in 1945; it is concerned with religious and cultural matters.

Please excuse me for bringing up these questions in the course of our celebration of the feast of Saint Stephen, patron saint of your parish. However, they are part of a logical line of thought which springs from Christ and his words to the Apostles, "Every one who acknowledges me before men, I also will acknowledge before my Father who is in heaven" (Matthew 10:32), and extends to our own days and to the Holy Year of 1975, which is now drawing to a close.

How shall we wind up this reflection? We could of course go into more detailed analysis of the facts, but we are limited by time. So how shall we finish?

While we are all gathered together here let us remember Saint Stephen and pray that each of you and also your bishop who is speaking to you may bear witness to Christ. Let us pray that each of us may profess his faith on the individual, community, and social levels. This is our prayer today.

Let us pray that our children may profess their faith in an increasingly mature way and in complete freedom—freedom we won through long years of slavery, partition, and terrible occupation. We have never betrayed Christ or our country and have won this vital freedom and right of the believing citizen to be respected in all areas of life.

So let us pray that our children may profess Christ in complete freedom, awareness, and maturity. Let us pray that our life in this country may be lived in accordance with all human rights, including respect for religious freedom and for freedom of conscience and speech, especially when social responsibilities are entailed.

May Saint Stephen, who bore witness to Christ and is the patron saint of this parish, intercede with the incarnate Word on behalf of our prayer. The Word became flesh and dwelt among us. He became flesh in the womb of the Virgin Mary and was born of her. The Word became flesh. The Word of God cannot be stifled.

26 December 1975

11

❧

The Feast of
Saint John the Evangelist

Today's gathering, when we share our special blessed bread with one another, harks back to our Christmas celebrations and particularly the ancient Christian tradition of our people for Christmas Eve. Moreover, since this tradition echoes the actions of the upper room, it should be particularly meaningful to us who ascend the altar every day. Christmas Eve is thus the inspiration for this meeting between you and your bishop here in this place where you so recently trained for the priesthood. It was I who ordained you to the priesthood, and in my heart I felt a strong wish to meet with you here and share this blessed bread with you.

Our gathering is even more meaningful today on the third day of the Christmas octave, which the Church has dedicated to Saint John the Evangelist. In this connection, I want to draw your attention to this saint and, after a brief reflection on today's readings, take this opportunity of giving you my Christmas greetings and wishes, which I have not been able to deliver until now.

Saint John the Evangelist was a man who lived Jesus Christ in a very special way. Of course each one of the apostles was with Jesus in his own individual way. Being an apostle means transmitting Christ's message to others, in other words bearing witness to him, not taking this from some indirect, exterior source, but drawing it directly from interior experience of him. All the apostles experienced Christ directly. However, Saint John the Evangelist described this experience, and we find his precious descriptions in his gospel and letters and in the book of Revelation.

We also find differences between his descriptions and those of Matthew, who was also an apostle but who wrote his gospel earlier and with a special eye on the requirements of the apostolate and also the circumstances in which he was living. John, on the other hand, wrote his gospel as a sort of retrospective account, which is why his narrative had been more meditated and was deeper and more expressive. Even today, the Gospel of Saint John still speaks to us at every turn of his experience of Christ.

Moreover, we know that Saint John, who was both apostle and evangelist, sometimes felt the need to emphasize his personal link with Christ. We find evidence of this in his reference to personal moments, when he speaks, for example, of the disciple "whom Jesus loved" (John 20:2) or, in his description of the Last Supper, his emphasis on the bond of affection between them.

In the tradition of the Church, Saint John is seen as the beloved disciple and as an especially sublime figure. His great purity, the transparency of his sentiments, and his simplicity are emphasized, so that he is placed on a level above the other apostles and is seen as an ideal, indicated to us by Christ himself as most clearly mirroring his person and teachings.

When the Church sets him before us in the Christmas octave, it is in a certain sense placing him within the context of the mystery of the Incarnation, close to the manger, since Saint John, with his special closeness to Christ, revealed the interior depths of Christ's being. He is the evangelist of the Word become flesh, and this is why his place in the liturgical year is so close to that of the Incarnation. He is the evangelist of love—and love is the fundamental expression of the Word who came among us and in whose name we gather as his disciples, his community, his Church.

This brief sketch of Saint John the Evangelist is a prelude to what I want to wish you, my dear priests, my young sons and my brothers in the priesthood, while we share the blessed bread: my prayer is that you may experience Christ unceasingly.

This was no doubt your aim when you entered the seminary and was the main motivation of your vocation. You wanted to draw close to Christ, and you chose the priesthood in order to do so.

Such a choice does of course entail other aims—as was the case in the lives of the apostles. However, the predominant one is always that encounter, and this is why you entered the seminary, even though the desire may not yet have been clearly articulated. Then the seminary taught you to experience Christ. Although it is not possible to teach this experience as a specific subject, it is possible to create a foundation for it and indicate the necessary preconditions. Every person (and every priest) must experience Christ in his own personal way, through his desire for Christ and his acceptance of him and his willingness to develop this within his soul through the dialogue of prayer.

What we learned in the seminary, with its crowning moment of ordination to the priesthood, must continue and develop within us, and if this does not happen, it is impossible to be a priest and to live the priesthood in a fruitful manner. Jesus taught us this at the Last Supper, as Saint John reports in his gospel: "No longer do I call you servants . . . but friends" (John 15:15). There are many other references to this subject, so that we are told how we must live for Christ, who we are in virtue of the priesthood, and what is the most important thing about the priesthood. Be that as it may, the essential aspect is friendship with Christ and experience of this, which is the fulcrum of the whole life of the priesthood and of its activity, service, and effectiveness.

You must look within yourselves and consider what experience you have had of Christ. Are you always filled with this experience or has it sunk into your subconscious, leaving nothing but activism and mechanical behavior—things that, without the fusion provided by Christ, make the priesthood simply an empty word? We all know that by its very nature the human mind is unable to remain concentrated exclusively on one single thing—in our case on Christ. However, it is easy to see whether what we do and how we live—indeed, our whole activity as priests—springs from it and is ordered toward it. Do we have an experiential link with Christ, or does it seem to have disappeared? My dear ones, we must be careful that this bond is not broken. We must make sure that we live ever more deeply in Christ, so that this bond constantly grows not so much quantitatively as qualitatively.

The best testing point for this is the Holy Mass. I may be celebrating Mass extremely correctly, but is this simply an external correctness? Or am I deeply aware of being the instrument to which Christ entrusts himself and his work? Entrusting oneself and one's work to other people indicates vast trust. His work is his self-giving to the Father for the salvation of every single person. Am I constantly aware that in a certain sense he is entrusting this work to me? When I preach the word of God, he entrusts me with his thought, his word. And when I give absolution—my dear ones, I know that listening and discerning is very tiring, since as men our capacities are limited—but, the Lord be praised, there are still long lines outside our confessionals. We must always remember who it is who has granted us priests the power to absolve and never forget that it was through the cross that he paid for the sins of each person and of all humanity.

The Council teaches us to look within ourselves and examine our interior lives as priests. Consider how you live and act, and ask yourselves if the experience of Christ is developing within you. If Christ is alive within us, then everything we do is quite different; it produces new results and is seen in a different light. People are not asking too much of us if they want to see Christ in us so that they can view each of us as an *alter Christus*. Of course this makes great demands on us, but, however great these demands, they are not impossible. We must live in Christ in such a way that people can see us as an *alter Christus*; otherwise, they will be disillusioned.

My dear ones, this is enough for now. This is a very serious and complex matter and could be developed at much greater length. However, I think that these few words are enough, since it is not new to you and you have even read about it in your breviaries today.

I hope that you may constantly live in Christ and that you may grow in this same experience as the apostles did. I hope that living in Christ may be the source of your priestly joy. We seek joy in every vocation and in the priestly vocation in a special way. I hope that the priesthood may never bring you disillusionment despite the many difficulties and obstacles of life, but that even in difficulty it may be the source of joy for you and the source of immense good for others and for the Church.

These are my wishes for you today, as we break bread together in accordance with our Christmas Eve tradition. May you ever live in Christ, our Lord and Master, and may this experience develop and deepen within you.

27 December 1969

12

❧

The Feast of the Holy Family

In the Christmas season we often address the newborn Lord with the prayer: "Raise your little hand, O Holy Child, and bless our beloved homeland."

However, today we are celebrating the feast of the Holy Family, when the Church asks Jesus to bless the family. May he, who was the blessing of his own family because he grew to manhood within it, preparing himself in its shelter for his messianic vocation, bless every human family. Today, the hope and fervent desire of the Church is that every human family may be permeated with the mystery of the Holy Family, in which God became man.

This mystery offers many points for reflection: Christ spent his childhood and youth with his family, thus showing us that God's greatest work is carried out within the family; he wrought our redemption and salvation in the context of his family life; and it is thanks to it that all of us are saved. This is why today's feast is of such universal significance. The light of the Holy Family shines out to anywhere where there is a human family—which in fact means everywhere.

The meaning of this feast is also very individual and personal. Today the mystery of the Holy Family concerns each individual family in a specific way—both husband and wife but also that special community which begins with their marriage, in other words, the community of parents and children. Whether this is a community of mature people or of those still in formation, it is a wonderful and fundamental community, and without it the human race would not exist.

In a special way today, through the mystery of the Holy Family, all humanity and the Church reflect on God's greatest work—that of creation. God started the human race when he created the first human couple of man and woman, husband and wife. The great human family began with them; when he gave them the power to transmit life, he invested them with the divine power of creation. Thus the work of creation continues through the family in every age and generation of human history. As parents, you are partners with God and share in his work in a way in keeping with the dignity of the human person. The Creator wants the work of creation to be manifested in every human family and, through the family, in every people and society and in humanity as a whole.

While this is a fundamental truth that can be explained also to non-Christians, inasmuch as it must be clear to everybody that humanity cannot exist without the family, for us Christians it is particularly important in the perspective of the work of redemption and sanctification that is carried out through the family. If the Son of God became man and carried out the major part of his mission within the family, this means that his work must be carried out within and through the family. This work of redemption and sanctification raises man up out of the evil to which he has inclined as a result of original sin and draws him toward the good of which he is capable, even at the price of effort and sacrifice. Jesus showed us this, and he urges us toward it, constantly giving us new strength for our task.

The work of redemption shows us the full value of everything human and especially of marriage and the family. It is as if God himself—symbolized in the family by every newborn child—said to every couple: "See how beautiful it is, and how it is both human and divine!" This is the meaning of today's feast.

The divine and human beauty that exists in the family can only be gained through constant effort. It is not ready-made, but must be worked for by every couple. We are quite right in saying that marriage is based on love; we find this truth in the gospel. However, we must immediately add that true love makes us capable of taking on the tasks and problems of married and family life and that if it does not give us this capacity it cannot be called love. We should therefore be careful not to debase this wonderful word that was spoken by the Son of God as the greatest commandment.

Through marriage and the family Christ carries out his work of redemption, which he won for us on the cross. However, just as Christ came to resurrection through the cross, so too, difficulties and hardship bring us to the true values of marital and family love and real formation and development—first and foremost the mutual formation of husband and wife and then the education of their children.

Only well-trained and formed adults are capable of educating the young. This is also part of the work of sanctification that flows from the mystery of the Holy Family through the sacrament of matrimony.

The Son of God became man within the family, and this is also why he made a sacrament of this primordial state which was instituted by his Father, our Creator. He made his call to husband and wife to create a marital and family community into a sacrament.

The deepest witness of this community is the institution of marriage. This can be seen clearly both in the Old Testament and also in all the words and actions of Christ. Since we are followers of Christ, living in accordance with the gospel, it is not licit for us to live in matrimony except in terms of this sacrament. Only a union permeated by the action of the Holy Spirit is in keeping with our condition as baptized Christians.

We have a right to the sanctification that comes from the sacrament of matrimony, but we also have the obligation of seeking the sanctity of matrimony. Let us not imagine that the sacrament of matrimony takes effect mechanically; no, it acts together with the will and efforts of the individual. The sacrament helps us and makes sanctification possible, but we, for our part, must demonstrate our goodwill and humbly pray. This is the only way of reaching sanctity, whether in the priesthood or in marriage.

My dear ones, these reflections are prompted by the mystery of the Holy Family and are of great importance to the Church, which always gives Christian matrimony and its sanctity a primary place in its mission because Christ founded the Church by beginning his mission as Messiah within the family.

Today we offer our wholehearted prayers in the words of our special Polish Christmas carol: "Raise your little hand, O Holy Child, and bless our beloved homeland." We pray for our country, in the knowledge that (as is the case for any country, people, or society) its strength lies in the family.

Too little is done to develop and harness this strength, while, on the contrary, a great deal is done to weaken the marriage bond and the stability of the family. The individual, the marriage, and the family should be given assistance; indeed, the state or society exists for this.

"Bless our homeland," this beloved country, whose fundamental strength lies in each individual family. And we must be careful that this strength does not become weakness and that we do not lose this underlying strength of every society and country.

While we can change the parts of an engine, the fundamental human community of the family cannot be substituted. It must be served and helped to develop. It is not licit to destroy it, since it is a work of God.

So let us pray: Bless our country!

Today, in the parish of Zakopane, we pray: Bless this parish that has chosen the Holy Family as its protector and enable it to draw a true family spirit from it.

"Raise your little hand, O Holy Child, and bless the family"— every family that is loved by its members and dear to other people and lives in the atmosphere of love. There is nothing dearer to man than this community.

"Bless the family; bless our country." We pray that every family in Poland, each one of which is a member of this wider parish family of humanity, may be pleasing to God.

This is the meaning of the Christmas prayer that we sing together around the manger in which the Holy Child lies. Together with you, and through the words of this Christmas carol, I invoke the blessing of the Holy Child for our country and for our families.

28 December 1969

13

❧

New Year's Eve

As we do each year, we have crowded into our churches in these last hours of 1966. When we are moving into a new phase of history and of our lives, we like to pause on the threshold and look back before continuing on our way.

However, this year our pause is rather different, since it must take in not just the past year but the whole thousand-year period of our Christian history to date and look to a future which offers great opportunities and challenges. Thus, the threshold of time on which we are pausing extends from this religious celebration to include the whole year.

We reflected on this one year ago, in this same marian basilica, when we announced the opening of the jubilee year marking a thousand years since the baptism of Poland. The whole year should have provided a threshold on which to pause and look carefully back so as to reconcile ourselves with the whole of the past.

When we speak of the past, we are not referring simply to what is dead; although this could apply in the strictly material order, it definitely does not do so in the human sphere. The past is always the beginning, the basis, and the framework for the future.

While moving toward the future, we must not cut ourselves off from the past so drastically but must integrate what has been with what is and what will be. The past is a sort of test or measure for the future to the extent that it will be able to shape it and give it its orientation.

This thousandth year since the birth of the Polish nation and its baptism has provided us with a special opportunity for reflection and self-examination. The history of the Polish people stretches from 966 to 1966; and a people is a society, or a family in the broader sense of the term since, although it does not actually give birth to new individuals, it does educate them in the constant unrolling of history. We can quite correctly say that each of us has been educated by the history of our people and the successes and failures of its thousand years, from its dawning with Mieszko I down to our own days. We cannot deny the truth of this, and it would be wrong of us to try to play down the importance of this historical perspective or deny our past, because this would mean impoverishing ourselves and diminishing the vast heritage that educates us both individually and collectively. This millenial year, this great jubilee year, has brought us to see the past in this perspective.

Looking back, we have realized the great values this past continues to have for us. Despite all the tragedies and misfortunes we have suffered, despite all the national weaknesses and defects of which we are so well aware, and despite all our failures and setbacks, this past has provided us with the framework for our future.

Each time during this year that we have looked back on these thousand years, we have clearly seen the living presence of Jesus Christ in the history of our ancestors. Even if we insisted on viewing this past with indifferent or hostile eyes, we would have to recognize this. All that is needed is a more benevolent or objective gaze in order to see irrefutable signs of the living presence of Christ in this land throughout the centuries. This presence has of course not been a physical one as it was in his own land two thousand years ago, but it has been just as effective through his gospel and sacraments. Although the word is not the whole man and the sacraments are only signs, together they constitute the living presence of Christ. This is the way in which he has chosen to be present among humanity, and this is the way in which he has been present among us for a thousand years.

This year we have knelt around our baptismal fonts, circled our altars with veneration, and paid special attention to the words of Christ's gospel. All this has confirmed his presence among us over the past thousand years and also in the present: a living presence among living people. It would be helpful if we could call up all those who have been filled with this presence and have them among us now, since if we looked at their lives and saw into the mystery of their souls, we would see to what an extent Christ had been present in them. However, since it is not possible to bring the dead back to life, we must simply look into the depths of our own souls, reflecting on the meaning of our lives, examining the joys and sorrows of our own consciences. We must reflect on our own hopes and fears and on the tensions in our interior struggles to see that Christ is living his own life among and within us.

Christ's presence in our history has been the subject of retrospective analysis and special reflection this year due to the fact that we are on the threshold of a new millenium. Two of the more outstanding dates for such reflection were 14 April, when all the bells in Poland were pealed to commemorate the probable day on which Mieszko and Poland received holy baptism, and 8 May, when the traditional centuries-old procession from Wawel to Sialka took place. (This is the procession in which the Polish kings used to take part—those same kings who are now in the Wawel crypt awaiting the resurrection.)

All this has given outward evidence of Christ's presence among and within us throughout the past millenium and has shown how for us his presence has been a great source of good, providing an inestimable historical heritage and a central value around which the history, not just of individuals but of the whole nation, has been formed. Christ has been the focal point around which we have been able to develop and the support on which to lever ourselves up after any fall. His word and sacrament and his presence among us have meant that hope has never failed, and we have loved the ideals that are based on the gospel and that today constitute the heritage of all mankind and underlie its progress. Brotherhood, love, and freedom have their roots in Christ, and we would be justified in seeing the fact that these ideals, truths, and values form the cornerstone of our millenial existence as evidence of the presence of Christ throughout the history of our nation.

It is necessary to consider all this now at the end of the year. Before moving into the future, we must clearly understand that these values, truths, and ideals have not been lost but have retained all their power intact. Providence has arranged for our millenial year to coincide with the Second Vatican Council, which has given fresh life to the words of Christ in the mind of the Church and of all humanity.

We should listen to these words carefully because they are in fact our spiritual heritage. At this point, I should like to cite just two of them: *freedom* and *dialogue*.

What does *freedom* mean? Freedom is a characteristic of the human person and forms part of human nature and of our right to an authentic existence that is neither weakened from within nor destroyed from without. Freedom is the right to an authentic existence and to truth, justice, and love—to all those things John XXIII spoke about in his encyclicals, especially the one dedicated to peace.* Freedom is also the right to society, and the Church is a society. The Church proclaims the principle of freedom to the modern world and thus, on the grounds of equal rights, demands freedom for itself of every individual of which this world is composed: freedom for its own communities, for its parishes, dioceses, and seminaries. This is one of the key words of the Council, which, thanks to the Council, have become Christ's words to this century.

The word *dialogue* is a correlate of the word *freedom* and refers to the basic tissue that builds up human relationships in every dimension (both international and those between persons or groups with different ideas) on the basis of the common search for truth. Dialogue cannot be a unilateral decree, nor can it be action on the part of a stronger party, taking advantage of its superior strength in order to undermine or diminish the authentic existence of the other. Dialogue is the fruit of freedom and works for it in relations between persons or nations. Dialogue is a source and guarantee of

---

Pacem in terris, 1963.

peace on every level. And the present pope appeals for dialogue in an attempt to save the modern world from the threat of war.

My dear ones, these are the words of the Church of this millenium, the words of the Church of the Council; they are the words of Christ who lives within and with humanity as its Redeemer.

Today we must examine the meaning of the year that has just ended so that we can integrate the past with the future. In this way we can move into the future without cutting ourselves off from the past but retaining our most precious human possessions, which are for this very reason divine.

My dear ones, we have gathered here in this venerable old shrine of the Virgin Mary. We have all gathered here—its bishop, together with the clergy, religious sisters, and laity—in order to render our final thanks in this millenial year, to sing one last Te Deum, and, so to speak, to link the past to the future. Our eyes and hearts turn to Christ and to his mother who, by giving birth to him, united the past with the future in him. The whole of the past has its focus in Christ, and the whole of the future has its source in him. In the course of this millenial year, we have renewed our baptismal vows before Our Lady in every church, including Wawel Cathedral, where this took place before the Jasna Gora icon, first at Easter and then during the jubilee celebrations. We have entrusted our past to her, just as we entrust our future to her, in the certainty that in her hands we shall stand firm and never yield in any way. We entrust the earthly existence of each one of us to her, since each human person is of inestimable value. And we entrust to her our spiritual existence and everything that constitutes the interior and primary content of our lives, so that our spiritual existence or interior life is not mired down or lost in the problems and ideological distortions of the times in which we are living and those to come.

Our trust is great, as are our faith and confidence in Mary's maternal closeness to our souls. Through this presence, may she unite our past and our future in Jesus Christ.

At this moment between one millenium and another, our thoughts turn to the generations that will follow us. Will they possess the same spirit that we have inherited from the thousand years of our existence? I am addressing this question to you, O Virgin Mother, because we are not able to answer it ourselves. I am addressing it to you as my own prayer—and as the prayer of all of us. Is there anything greater and better for us to pass on to our descendants than the divine heritage that your Son brought us?

So, on the threshold of a new era, we pray to you, O Mother of our Redeemer, that through your hands, your heart, and your motherhood, the heritage of your Son may be passed on to those who will call themselves Poles after we have left this earth. May this heritage become their possession, their heritage, their truth, their freedom, and the basis of their existence in this world and the next.

31 December 1966

14

❦

New Year's Day:
The Feast of Mary, Mother of God

Although we are only at the beginning of a new year, our thoughts, strange to say, turn to the beginning of time itself, and we try to see this fleeting moment of human history as if we were at the beginning of time and were standing before the eternal One who, in his omnipotence, is the source of the whole of creation, which is then subject to time.

In these first moments of the new year, let us stand before God, who is the Creator of our very existence and the Lord of time. Let us render him glory and raise up to him that hymn of praise which time, and, within time, all of creation, and, within the world of creation, man, express and proclaim imperfectly and which the eternal Son of the eternal Father expresses perfectly in a manner worthy of God.

Our thoughts and hearts turn to Christ, and we meditate on the eternal Word who is of one substance with the Father and is, like him, omnipotent and eternal but who subjected himself to time, becoming flesh within time and coming to live among us. We enter into this new period of time, this new year, in his name, since this name was given to us on earth for our salvation. The name of Jesus Christ means salvation for all people and forms the history of human salvation or history seen as a temporal question that concerns man within time.

So the man who was Son of God entered into time and permeated human time with divine salvation. This new year of 1969 in human history is a new year in the history of our salvation. We count our years from the birth of Christ and link them to his name and hence to all the salvific power of the name Jesus Christ. This is why we are living the first moments of the new year within the heart of this power. For what is the Holy Mass if not Christ himself who unceasingly offers himself to his own Father and who is above time; Christ who, in his unceasing self-giving to the Father, binds himself to each of us as an individual and to mankind as a whole; Christ who makes us one with himself and offers us to the Father as his mystical body?

Thus, in these first moments of the new year of Our Lord 1969, we enter into the power of Jesus Christ and anchor our time, our existence, our offering, and our destiny in him. In these first moments of the new year, together with him we make our offering to our common Father, who is beyond all time, just as we shall make it every day of this year.

We do not know what will happen in this period, so that it is, so to speak, a frame for an unknown future. However, we do know that the threads of the power named Jesus stretch forward from this first moment of the new year and that within this power we can find a place for our problems, since the whole human family with all its problems has its place there.

We are now expressing this here at the altar. The first day of the new year is dedicated to prayer for world peace, a cause very dear to the heart of the Holy Father. He has invited us to consecrate the first day of the new year to prayer for peace on earth—that peace which was proclaimed over the Bethlehem stable when God entered into human time and became man as Jesus Christ. Let us therefore wholeheartedly meet the Holy Father's call and dedicate this first day of the new year to world peace by adding our fervent prayers to his.

On this world day of prayer for peace, Pope Paul VI has asked for special emphasis to be given this year to the question of respect for human rights. This path to peace was also emphasized by Pope John XXIII, of venerated memory, in his unforgettable encyclical

Pacem in terris. If peace is to reign on earth, favorable conditions for this must be created among men. The first of these is respect for the various human rights, which were listed by John XXIII in this encyclical: the right to truth, the right to freedom, the right to justice, the right to love. If we are to pray for peace in the spirit of John XXIII's encyclical and in conformity with the intentions of Paul VI on the first day of this new year, we must all pray together that human rights should be respected in every part of the world and that this should be done in practice (and not just set forth in charters or constitutions) because this is what public and social life needs.

The path to peace goes by way of the person with recognition of his dignity and respect for the rights that spring from this dignity. The Church shows all humanity the path to peace; it is that same path which the Prince of Peace, Jesus Christ, showed humanity on that first night in Bethlehem and continues to show us, particularly at Christmas time each year. This is the path we must take, which is why all of you, on this first day of the new year, should respond to Paul VI's call and pray that all mankind—every nation, society, social system, and government—may follow this sole path of peace that has been shown to us by Jesus Christ, who is constantly reborn in his Church, this path that entails the protection and enlargement of human rights. The Holy Child has been born for us! This Child bears special power on his shoulders because he is the king of every age; however, even more than power, in his heart he bears the cross of all humanity. Through the centuries, may the divine Child restore and uphold our human rights with this cross, bringing greatness, dignity, holiness, and peace for men of goodwill.

1 January 1969

* * *

"At every minute, in every hour, for all eternity, may he be praised!" With the words of this hymn we saw the old year draw to its close, and we commended every minute and hour to Jesus in the trust that in him, who is our love, every minute enters into eternity. As man, Christ is subject to time in the form of minutes, hours, and years; however, as God, he is free of time, since he is bound, so to speak, to the dimension of eternity.

From the human viewpoint it is, in fact, incorrect to speak of minutes and hours in eternity because eternity has neither minutes nor hours but is outside time; it is God's dimension or characteristic, whereas human time is counted in minutes, hours, days, years, and eras. We have just finished one period of human time. We wanted to dedicate the last words we sang to him since we meant to spend those last moments of the year (as we tried to do throughout every hour of the whole year) with him, so as to start the new one, which began a few minutes back, with him.

"In every minute of every hour"—of this first hour and of all the hours in the year and of all the days, weeks, and months to come. Let us offer all of them to him now in advance, without knowing how much of this time will be ours or to what extent it will belong to each of us. The future, as represented by the new year, is unknown to us since it lies in the hands of God. Let us leave it there with him!

We begin it with Jesus Christ because he is the beginning of all the years marked on the calendar of time—our calendar, that of all peoples, and that of all humanity. In our calendar all these years are counted from the day of his birth; although it may not be very accurate in the chronological sense, this does not mean that it is any less bound to him in the ideal sense. "The common era," as profane usage would have it; "anno Domini" (year of Our Lord), as Christian usage has specified for centuries.

So we have begun the year of Our Lord 1978. He is the beginning of the new year, which will from now on appear in our calendars and newspapers. He is the beginning.

The beginning of the new year is quite rightly linked to the Christmas celebrations, which last for one week and then today, on the eighth day, culminate in the special feast of Mary's motherhood, through which God, who is eternal and unlimited by time, entered into time and became man, thus ushering in the new age. We therefore venerate Mary's motherhood so as to see Christ more fully as our beginning. Everything began from him, who is without beginning: "In the beginning was the Word, and the Word was with God, and the Word was God" (John 1:1).

Even though a great deal of time—many years, centuries, and whole ages—preceded his coming (and contemporary science has discovered that there have been millions of years since the beginning of the world, and even since man's beginnings within it), everything had its true origins in him and his birth. It is through his birth that human time—the time of the world and of all creatures—regained its own true meaning, inasmuch as creatures, the world, time, and the human race are all oriented toward God.

We begin this new year through him, with him, and in him. Meanwhile, we gaze with immense veneration at her who enables us, year after year, to begin a new life with him and to move towards a future that is humanly unknown but that with him, in him, and through him, constitutes a time and path of salvation and enables us to move toward God.

Thus, my dear brothers and sisters, we begin this new year in the name of Jesus Christ, celebrating the Eucharist so that right from the very first hour it may be imbued with this mystery which unites him to all of us.

Let us also remember that here in Poland, 1978 is the third year of preparation for the six-hundredth anniversary of the icon of Our Lady of Jasna Gora. Again in Poland and especially in Krakow, it is also the eighth year of preparation for the nine-hundredth anniversary of Saint Stanislaus, bishop and martyr, who is patron saint of our country. These great centenaries involve not only our past history but also our future. They concern the history of the days and years to come and will bring new vitality to the Church, and also to the whole population of this country.

Lastly, let us remember that each year 1 January is the day of peace. Christ, the octave of whose birth we are celebrating, is peace and brings peace: "My peace I give to you; not as the world gives do I give to you" (John 14:27).

Following the wishes of the Holy Father, we pray each year that the whole world, at least to some extent, may share in the peace which Christ gives us. Let us pray for peace! This year the Holy Father's new year message of peace is brief and to the point: *no* to the abuse of power; *no* to violence; and *yes* to peace. This message is meant for us too, in that we must, in all freedom, have the strength of children of God as described by Saint John in the first chapter of his gospel; this strength is different from—indeed, the opposite of—violence and the abuse of power.

When the Holy Father says no to the abuse of power, he means that each person must be aware of his own rights—the rights to truth, love, justice, and freedom—because they constitute our true strength; and human and social life throughout the world and in Poland must be built on this strength rather than on the use of force.

This is why the Holy Father says yes to peace. When the life of the human person is shaped in accordance with the fundamental rights to truth, justice, freedom, and love, it unfolds peacefully, and peace becomes a true condition and reality.

At the beginning of the year let us pray that each person on earth—and especially in Poland—may have that strength which ensures peace, and that peace may guarantee the rights of each person and thus guarantee this strength.

These are the wishes of the Holy Father, and ours must echo them in these first hours of the new year if this first day is truly to be a festival of peace.

We greet this new year around the manger of Jesus Christ in the Christmas octave by raising our voices in Christmas carols and with the hope which Jesus brings us with his birth. As we celebrate the holy sacrifice, let us pray that throughout the whole of this year Christ may let us share in his mystery: "At every hour of the day, on every day of the week, and in every month of the year, may he be ever praised!"

1 January 1978

* * *

On this first day of the year, which is the last of the Christmas octave, the Church venerates the motherhood of Mary. We might say that the first day of the Christmas octave (that is, the feast itself) is filled with adoration of the divine fatherhood. The Holy Mass of that day places special emphasis on the mystery of the eternal fatherhood of God: fatherhood/sonship, eternal Father/eternal Son. In the mystery of Christmas human nature comes to share in this relationship: the Word becomes flesh; God becomes man.

A virgin gives birth to him as man, and today, at the close of the Christmas octave, the Church looks especially to this virgin and her motherhood.

We too, in accordance with the mind of the Church, try to concentrate our hearts around the mystery of Mary's divine motherhood, especially as the source of the Holy Family. A family begins with the maternity of the mother, and maternity with the conception of the child. When a woman conceives a child she becomes a mother, sharing in the mystery of motherhood and, in the human dimension, enabling her husband to attain the dignity of fatherhood. In human history this has always been the situation regarding this basic, eternal, and unchanging question.

Mary's motherhood was different, in that her pregnancy was virginal, beginning at the moment when the Archangel Gabriel brought her the heavenly Father's message: "You will conceive and bear a son." Immediately, with an instinctive reaction of mind and heart, Mary asked: "How can this be, since I have no husband?" The archangel answered: "The Holy Spirit will come upon you. . . . The child to be born of you will be called holy, the Son of God" (Luke 1:31–35).

This is how Mary's motherhood began. With these words she conceived within her the Word of God. With them the Word was conceived and took on a body ("The Word became flesh"). This event was hidden from the eyes of others and remained a secret in Mary's heart. When she heard the words of the archangel, she showed total obedience to the will of the heavenly Father and said: "Let it be to me according to your word."

As the Fathers of the Church point out, Mary's maternity was also a long-awaited event—awaited not only by Israel, the people of God of the Old Testament, who looked for the promised Messiah, but also by the whole of humanity and all creation. One of the Fathers of the Church wrote: "All of creation waits for your answer, O Virgin, for your obedient acceptance." Although it was completely hidden, this was the true dimension of the event in which the Virgin of Nazareth became the Mother of God. Nor could it have been otherwise, since the Incarnation of the Word was the supreme event for all of creation. This was especially so for humanity, as the culmination and fulfillment of that for which we were created and chosen. Mary's motherhood embraces all this.

The Church rightly links the first day of the year with the mystery of the maternity of the Mother of God, since this maternity is the beginning of the new age—of all the new years we celebrate after Christ's birth. This date is decisive in the spiritual history of humanity since it marks the fulfillment of the eternal promise and, through him who was born of the Virgin, the beginning of this in each person.

However, when we reflect on the mystery of Mary's motherhood, we cannot forget that people completely disregarded her state. There was no room for her in the inn, and doors were shut in her face so that she was forced to the outskirts and treated as a nuisance. The long-awaited motherhood, which was the fulfillment of God's eternal promise and the hope of every creature and all humanity, was shut out by many people as something bothersome and unwelcome. Mary's divine maternity underwent this indignity on Christmas night.

Thus the joy of giving birth to the Son of God was mixed with sadness at her rejection and the lack of a proper shelter. It seemed that everything was going wrong, whereas the Son of God's coming into the world had been expected under quite different circumstances.

We should meditate frequently on Mary's motherhood. In my opinion, we in Poland feel particularly close to this event; our religious sense is marian, so that motherhood holds a special place in it. We could even go so far as to say that is is concerned more with Mary's motherhood than with the mystery of God the Father. But what is Mary's motherhood if not the royal road that leads to the mystery of God himself? From the beginning the Father filled her whole life, and she was always obedient to him from the first "Be it unto me" to the foot of the cross.

May Mary's motherhood be the source of many new reflections within the lives of Polish families. The life of every family begins with motherhood, and this beginning can be fraught with difficulties, so that the maternity of our Polish mothers is often overshadowed by sadness. This is something that I would prefer not to mention here but that makes pregnancy and childbearing within Polish families even more difficult today. The thing I prefer not to mention is the source of great suffering for many women, mothers, and families. There was even a period in which abortion was viewed almost as a duty, and mothers who decided to have a third or fourth child were frowned upon—and this could happen again today.

When we reflect on how Mary's maternity was despised and rejected on Christmas night and wonder about the reasons, we can maybe find the explanation in the fact that from the beginning the Son of God wanted to undergo all the sufferings that would afflict the childbearing of women and share in the experience of every rejected, undesired, and despised maternity. However, we must never forget that despising means murdering, using "scientific methods" to destroy a defenseless being before birth. This is a terrible disgrace for science. We must now consider what precisely has been destroyed in men and women. What has been killed within the mother? What has been destroyed in the family? And how much distrust has been created within it? Children's first trust, which is toward their own parents, comes from the fact that they were generated by them; it is trust of those who gave them life, rather than taking it. What will happen in a society in which this takes place? The effects are bound to be incalculable.

My dear brothers and sisters, we should not be blinded by the great advances that have been made in the field of productivity and technology when we are deprived of similar advances in the strictly human field of parenthood and childbearing.

On the first day of the new year the Church proclaims this great and fundamental truth to us, and we should reflect on it because it is essential to our whole personal, family, and national life.

Although childbearing has painful aspects, it is full of joy because a new human being is coming into the world. Let us therefore rejoice for the many children born in the year that has just drawn to a close and for those to be born in the one that is now beginning. Let us rejoice for the birth of the Son of God; let us rejoice because, in a certain sense, all these Polish mothers have given birth, give birth, and will give birth to him, extending the mystery of his birth within time. Today is not only the last day of the Christmas octave; nor is it only the feast of the old and new years. It is the celebration of the mystery of Christmas that extends within time and permeates the life of each individual and all humanity from its very first moments. When the Son of God became man within the Virgin's womb and was born on Christmas night, he made us children of God, through the grace of holy baptism.

My dear brothers and sisters of the parish of Zakopane, your pastor rightly emphasized earlier on that this is a most important year in the history of Zakopane and of this parish. It marks the fourth centenary of the founding of this town, which is now known throughout Poland and the whole world. So I want to conclude my reflections on the new year by expressing my best wishes for Zakopane. It has a special heritage, and your pastor has already spoken of this; it has contributed to the life of the nation and the Church and played its part in the struggle for independence. However, all this is in the past.

Today Zakopane is a tourist resort to which more and more foreigners flock, so that one hears more foreign languages and less of the old mountain dialect. At the beginning of this new year, which marks the four-hundredth anniversary of Zakopane, let us pray that the fine old traditions and Christian heritage of your area and parish are never disregarded or suppressed in favor of others. You must be careful about this and work with commitment for it. Thus my wishes for you at the beginning of Zakopane's jubilee year are these: may you be blessed by Christ Jesus, Son of the Most Blessed Virgin Mary; may the hearts of Poles turn to her who will always be the mother of our nation.

1 January 1978

15

❧

The Feast of the Epiphany

I want to give my greetings and those of the cathedral chapter to the representatives of our city and of the various parishes of Krakow who have gathered here to celebrate the feast of the Epiphany. This is the first opportunity I have had of greeting you in the year which has just begun.

As the community of the people of God in Krakow, we have also gathered here in order to exchange our new year's greetings and to pass on all the warmest sentiments the mystery of Christmas has given rise to within our hearts. Over a number of years this practice has become an Epiphany tradition for us.

In our country today the whole Church sings those most expressive lines: "O wise men from afar, O kings, where are you going in such haste?" These simple words, which even young children sing, evoke not only the historical event we have just read about in the Gospel of Saint Matthew, but also one of the deepest truths about man—that of his incessant search for God. "O wise men from afar, O kings, where are you going in such haste?"

Their journey from the countries of the East to Jerusalem and finally to Bethlehem parallels the human journey. Whatever the age, culture, civilization, or nation, people are always searching for God. Like the wise men, they glimpse him through the eyes of faith, and then they set forth in faith in the desire to draw closer to him in whom they believe and come to him in the eternal Bethlehem. However, if they have not found him through faith, in looking for the truth they seek this faith, and so seek God. As Saint Augustine put it: "I would not have sought you, if I had not already found you." Before starting to seek God, each person has in fact found him in a particular value that then provides the basic starting point for a further search.

"O wise men from afar, O kings, where are you going in such haste?" This is a symbolic expression of our interior human desire and of our seeking for faith. This desire and this search do not mean some empty journey; rather, they are the path which leads to encounter as is emphasized in today's feast. Man's movement toward God and his search for him constitute the fundamental truth about our human existence and are the measure of our greatness.

Of course we do sometimes meet people who claim that they do not know how to search or what to look for—just as there are others who have in fact had the grace of finding God but who, even so, have lost him through lack of commitment and care. All this is part of the truth about the human soul and about human history, both past and present. We seek God because we bear his image within ourselves; since we were created in the image and likeness of God, only in him can we find our real fulfillment and our final destiny.

In October 1974 I took part in the synod of bishops that met in Rome to consider evangelization in the modern world. This gathering gave us a wonderful overview of this fundamental truth about man in every part of the world and in every historical, cultural, religious, and social circumstance. Wherever man may be, he uses every means at his disposal to seek God, and those taking part in the synod, who had come from every part of the world (Asia, Africa, Europe, the Americas, Australia), testified to this. However, they also emphasized that this aspiration, which is the true path to evangelization, meets with varying obstacles, depending on continent, type of society, past history, and present conditions. This is of course normal for the gospel, and the Church reminds us of this in the Christmas period when we meditate on him who was born in Bethlehem as a sign of contradiction. We ourselves can understand it more clearly when we consider the many difficulties the wise men from the East had to undergo before reaching their destination in their encounter in Bethlehem.

If the search for God involves us who believe, those who do not believe but who sincerely seek the truth, and also those I mentioned who are not able to find it although they do intensely seek everything which augments true humanity and highlights human greatness, then from the viewpoint of human dignity it is impossible to accept atheism as the basis of any political system. We can understand the person who seeks but does not find and even the person who denies God; however, we simply cannot find any justification for denying others the right to believe with such attitudes as: "Do you want a job? Do you want a successful career? Then you must not believe, or you must hide your beliefs." From the viewpoint of human development and values, basing the existence of a state on atheism constitutes a painful error. Respect for the person is the primary precondition for any type of social life and equality between citizens.

I am talking about this today on the feast of the Epiphany because I can sense a type of anxiety that pervades our entire society and especially that part of it which believes. The vast majority of the population of Poland is made up of believers, and they have every reason to be afraid that atheism might become, either directly or indirectly, the basis of the existence of the state, suppressing our right to define ourselves and act in accordance with our convictions.

We cannot keep silent about such questions of social morality which cause anxiety in our hearts. We bishops, priests, and other believers cannot take these matters lightly. However worthy it may consider itself, one sector of society cannot impose on the whole population an ideology and world view which go against the beliefs of the majority. These are matters of vital importance.

My dear brothers and sisters, it may not be pleasant to dwell on such things during a new year's gathering. We came here to exchange greetings and wishes—and this is indeed what we intend doing. However, this is also precisely why I am talking about such things, because this whole situation is the subject of the wishes which are most important for Polish believers and thus for the whole community of the Krakow church to whom I am speaking today so that my wishes will be framed in the perspective of this question. Following Epiphany tradition, in a few moments we shall bless gold, frankincense and myrrh and also the sticks of chalk with which the three letters *G M B** will be written on the doors of our houses in memory of the three wise men from the East, about whom we are told in today's Gospel and about whom our Christmas carols sing. These three letters are not simply some empty tradition but indicate those three people who reached Christ and the fullness of revelation, so that they have become the model for all future generations of believers. We Polish believers also see them as our model, and this is why we write *G M B* on our doors together with the year 1976 indicating that, like them, we want to acknowledge Christ who was born in Bethlehem and accept the light of revelation. Like the three wise men we believe, and we want to live our faith in every sphere of our personal, family, social, and national life.

Nobody has the right to deny us this, even in formal terms. Poland is made up of believers and nonbelievers, and the latter cannot take decisions about its orientation, to the detriment of the former. Poland is not some casual agglomeration: Poland means a thousand years of history; it means Wawel with this cathedral and these royal tombs; it means the victories and sufferings we have experienced. We should remember that the sufferings of the Polish people are what won our first and second independence, which is why the people constitute the foundation of the existence of the state.

So my greetings and wishes go out to every person, to every believer, and to every seeker that they may believe and seek without being told that this is not allowed and that they may write *G M B* on the doors of their houses without being afraid that someone might hold this against them or threaten their position because of it.

Our greetings go out to every family, that they may bring up their children according to their Christian faith. We do not interfere in

---

*Caspar (or Gaspar), Melchior and Balthazar, the names traditionally given to the three magi.

the families of atheists since this concerns their own conscience; however, we cannot help but wish that Christian families in this country might send their children to school without the fear that a materialistic view of the world and an atheistic ideology will be forced on them.

The principles of freedom of conscience and freedom of religion must be interpreted in their full breadth. Freedom of conscience and religion is—as is affirmed by the Second Vatican Council, the Universal Declaration of Human Rights approved by the United Nations, and the Helsinki Accords—an inalienable human right which must never for any reason be abrogated or suppressed. None of the conditions of social life and of the existence of the state must erode this right; in public life there must not be privileges for non-believers and disadvantages for believers. Together we make up Poland; we all want to help develop it because we love it as the country in which we grew up. And Christians, who make up the great majority of the population, cannot be treated as second-class citizens simply because of their beliefs.

These are my wishes. You must forgive me if I have not formulated warm, conventional greetings; however, my wishes do come from the depths of the heart of a bishop who is concerned for every single person in his Church and country. I am concerned for every person, every family, and every parish, especially for parishes like Wzgórze Krzeslawickie and Osiedle Podwawelskie that have for years been exposed to the elements and living in the midst of mud because they have not been granted permission to build a church. How much longer will this problem be with us?

"O wise men from afar . . . Fierce anger persecutes the Child." This Christmas carol dedicated to the Epiphany of Our Lord proclaims a great truth. We know that Herod's anger has not come to an end. "Fierce anger persecutes the Child. . . . Herod is preparing a plot." How many Herods there have been in the course of history! We know that the persecuted Child is the Lord of our hearts and souls and that every persecution directed against his followers unites them ever more deeply with him, who will in the end be seen as the Way, the Truth and the Life. He came to us not in power and might but in a manger and on the cross. This is how, once for all time, he won every person who is in search of the truth and who believes in love.

"Thrice happy wise kings, who would not envy you?" Thrice happy wise kings—happy because they have reached the Bethlehem manger and found what they sought, happy because they have received the light of revelation, and happy in their faith.

This is the main point about today's feast. We meet together here, united in the joy of faith, the joy of Bethlehem, the joy of having received Christ. This joy will maybe be paid for with some material loss, for example a successful career; but this simply means giving up something in return for everything Christ has given for us.

We are reunited here in the joy of faith, which we share with many other people in different continents and of different races. What a great grace it is that our African brothers are growing in faith and in the community of the Church! Last year we had the Archbishop of India among us to represent a very great culture and also a bishop from Black Africa. Such representatives come to visit us for very special reasons. Do you know why Poland enjoys prestige throughout the world? It is because the world sees how Poland respects each individual's beliefs with his interior truth, conscience, and religion. It sees how the Poles, as a people and as a society, safeguard this respect in their attitudes, seeing their heritage as the possession of an atmosphere in which the person is accepted as being truly human.

So my wishes for you, my Poland, are that you may continue to enjoy this prestige throughout the world. I pray that you may enjoy the respect of the whole world for your sufferings and struggles, for the spiritual maturity of your children and the attitude of your Christians, for the faithfulness of your Church, and for the union which exists between bishops, priests, religious, and laity. May you remain an example for all the peoples of the world!

O my country, please accept these wishes which come to you from the bishop of Krakow, the guardian of Wawel with its national memories and historical monuments, the spokesman for our great tradition, and the successor of Saint Stanislaus!

O my Poland, please accept these wishes I am addressing to you at the beginning of 1976. Let us pray together, my dear brothers and sisters, that this year may be blessed by the Holy Child of Bethlehem. "Raise your little hand, O Holy Child, and bless our beloved homeland!"

6 January 1976

16

ॐ

The Feast of the Baptism of the Lord

For centuries the Church has linked the mystery of the revelation of God's coming to the feasts of Christmas and the Epiphany. Indeed, while for us the Epiphany recalls principally the arrival of the three magi in Bethlehem, in the tradition and liturgy of the Eastern Church these celebrations are extended to include Christ's baptism in the Jordan.

If we look back on this event, it is easy to see how fully it manifests the mystery of God's self-revelation. Although Christmas night does contain this mystery in its fullness, those taking part in it have a somewhat limited knowledge of it. The Bethlehem shepherds who are called to the stable are simple witnesses of the fulfillment that night of the promises made to the chosen people of the Old Testament; the special spirit and atmosphere of Christmas spring from their simplicity and spontaneous joy. The three wise men from the East who come to the same stable are more explicitly looking for the Messiah; their conversation with Herod and the doctors of the law, after which they continue to Bethlehem, indicates that even people outside the Old Testament tradition are illuminated by the ray of light coming from God's truth, which was announced by the prophets, so that they hope for the Messiah as the fulfillment of this truth. Thus in a certain way today's feast fully reveals the mystery of the Messiah.

The word *messiah* means "one who has been anointed with oil." Anointing, which played a great role in the Old Testament and is continued even today in the sacraments of the New Covenant, was symbolic in nature; in other words, it indicated something else beyond itself. The Scriptures make no mention of any similar anointing in Christ's case, even though the Messiah is the one proper subject of that which such anointing symbolizes. This "anointing with the Holy Spirit" (to use the expression of Saint Peter as found in today's reading from the Acts of the Apostles [10:38]) is manifested at the moment of his baptism in the Jordan.

The three wise men from the East were seeking the reality of this anointing although they were not aware of the fact. However, there was one man of the Old Covenant who did reach it: John, the son of Zechariah and Elizabeth.

The moment of revelation, or epiphany, which he experienced and in which we share through him, is therefore all the more striking. John, who had a purely monotheistic view of the one, incomprehensible God, became the bridge between the Old and New Covenants; but first and foremost he became the man of the Messiah's self-revelation, when Jesus, the Son of Mary, whom he had known since childhood, came to the Jordan to be baptized by him.

John knew that the baptism he gave was only a baptism of repentance and of man's conversion to God. He also knew that Jesus, the Son of Mary, who was asking for baptism, had no need of repentance and conversion. And for this reason he refused to baptize him.

This awareness that Jesus was above the baptism of repentance was expressed by John with the prophetic revelation of "baptism in the Spirit": "He will baptize you with the Holy Spirit and with fire" (Matthew 3:11).

Against the background of John's awareness, the Messiah's self-revelation, which is linked by the liturgy to the mystery of Christmas, came to its fullness at the moment of his baptism in the Jordan. Chronologically speaking, this event took place thirty years after that Bethlehem night and also after the period of hidden life in which the aspect of revelation was, so to speak, suspended until the next sign. Today the Church returns to these signs, linking them into a single chain and celebrating this aspect as an integrated whole.

In his baptism in the Jordan, Christ manifests himself fully as Messiah and reveals God in the mystery of the Most Holy Trinity.

Indeed, immediately after the baptism, John and those who were present saw the event in a supernatural light, so that it was clear that the same Jesus who was coming out of the waters of the Jordan was the Son of God: "This is my beloved Son, with whom I am well pleased" (Matthew 3:17). It could also be seen that the relationship between Father and Son is a bond in the Holy Spirit—in that Spirit which Christ not only receives but which he has come in order to give to others.

John, a man of the Old Covenant, who had grown up in the tradition of the indivisible God Jahweh, had this awareness. He realized this truth at the moment of Jesus' baptism, receiving it from the one he was baptizing; in that event his prophecy concerning him who would baptize with the Holy Spirit was fulfilled.

The predictions about Emmanuel and the Messiah played a major role in the writings of the Prophets, especially Isaiah. *Emmanuel* means "God with us," and when Christ emerged from the waters of Jordan, this became clear.

He is also Emmanuel, or "God with us," in the sense that God fills us with the Holy Spirit. This is also the real meaning of the baptism of Jesus Christ: it makes us children of God, sharers in the divine nature. In other words, it extends the action of the Holy Spirit (who is in him and who led him to the Jordan) in every person who, through faith and the sacraments, will be his brother, disciple, and witness.

My dear brothers and sisters, here we truly have the fullness of the mystery of the manifestation or revelation that the liturgies of both the Western and Eastern churches link to the mystery of Christmas. During the various feast days and Sundays the liturgy has led us ever deeper into the mystery and experience of revelation, which has become clearer and clearer to us from the moment of birth onward.

Please excuse the complexity of these explanations. I may have been overly brief, but the problem is probably connected more with the fact that I am speaking not of something human but of a divine matter, so that it transcends human means of knowledge, understanding, and expression.

"Father, your only Son revealed himself to us by becoming man. May we who share his humanity come to share his divinity." Although what we ask in the opening prayer of today's liturgy is very simple, it is totally new and is a result of the mystery which has been experienced. Christ came to the Jordan in order to give birth to the new order, so that we would be inwardly transformed by him who is "of one substance with the Father" and of whom the Father stated, "This is my Son" but who became outwardly similar to us.

So there is similarity and dissimilarity. The indication of the dissimilarity is the Holy Spirit and the divinity of the Son, while that of the similarity is his humanity. This divine sonship and the Holy Spirit are what provide the basis and possibility of interior transformation for us human beings. In our human dimension we are called to divine life through grace and through the action of the Holy Spirit within us.

When the recent synod of bishops held in October was reflecting on the evangelization of the modern world, this question was raised.

If our task is to proclaim the gospel in an active and credible way and if we want to transform people in its spirit and light, then our action must be carried out in the Holy Spirit. It must be an extension of that baptism in the Spirit which was revealed at the Jordan: "He will baptize you with the Holy Spirit and with fire."

This is why, in its plan for the evangelization of the modern world, the synod emphasizes both life in the Spirit (and hence the interior life, prayer, and contemplation) and also theology and catechesis, when these are viewed as greater understanding and interiorization of the gospel (or the revelation of the mystery) and as the initiation of the human mind and will into the divine life and order.

Everything that springs from the Spirit and that shapes the human spirit contributes to man's interior resemblance to Christ, the Son of God, and to truly making us all children of God and bringing us to resemble the God-Man, the only-begotten Son of God.

The practical result of all this is not so much external conformity as the integrated development of Christian practice and behavior.

The synod calls us first and foremost to this interiorization and development.

While we share in the Eucharist on the feast of the baptism of Jesus in the Jordan, which the Church celebrates as the last act in the great liturgical cycle of the Incarnation and Epiphany, we ask that, through the Holy Spirit, we too may share ever more fully in the divine mysteries, and in particular in that of the divine sonship, which is by far the most important one for us. We also pray that, through our lives, we may also bring knowledge of this mystery to others.

12 January 1975

* * *

My dear brothers and sisters, today's gospel, which we have just heard, brings us to the River Jordan and tells us of the unique historical event of Jesus' baptism.

We know that John the Baptist lived and preached on the banks of the Jordan in the period prior to the coming of Jesus with his teaching and public ministry. This is why he is brought to our attention on various occasions during Advent, at Christmas, and today on the feast of Our Lord's Baptism. In Advent he is the forerunner and messenger of our Redeemer, calling us to prepare the way for the Lord Jesus. Today we see him as Baptist, administering the baptism of repentance, which is different from the sacrament instituted by Jesus.

When he baptized people, John called them to repentance and urged them to interior conversion to God. All those who came to be baptized by him saw this action as a sign of repentance, and they did truly repent. However, today that baptism of repentance is transformed into the baptism of revelation. Jesus has no need of repentance when he comes to John the Baptist. He comes, rather, to transform human repentance into divine grace with the baptism of revelation. Thus he reveals himself to John and his disciples and listeners, and the Holy Trinity itself bears witness to it. This revelation tells us that the baptism of repentance is transformed into the baptism of revelation, pointing the way to the baptism of grace that will be established by the Redeemer.

It was necessary that he who represents grace and salvation for us and who brings every sinner and penitent onto the path of divine grace should appear in the context of the baptism given by John.

My dear brothers and sisters, when considered in the perspective of Christmas, today's feast becomes even more expressive, commemorating, as it does, the baptism of Jesus in the Jordan. Each year the liturgical cycle in this period gives us a fresh look at the mystery of the Incarnation, in which God became man and revealed himself to us, thus enabling us to draw closer to him.

On the occasion of the feast of the Holy Family (to which this parish is dedicated), and in view of my presence, your parish priest invited to this gathering all those sick parishioners who are able to come to church, while those who cannot move will be visited in their homes, so that Christ, who is the life of our souls and of the whole Church, can be brought to them too.

I address myself to you, my brothers and sisters, whether you have been able to come here or not and to those generous souls who look after you—the parish helpers who dedicate themselves to the sick, the suffering, and those who have been abandoned, thus rendering a great service to Jesus, since, as he said, "As you did it to one of the least of these my brethren, you did it to me" (Matthew 25:40). He is with those who need help and also with those who provide this assistance. Christ is present among us in our loving actions toward our neighbor and in our charitable service. He comes to us, as he did then, in order to transform the baptism of repentance into the baptism of revelation and grace.

My dear brothers and sisters, this is the special secret of your existence: suffering, abandonment, and loneliness are like the baptism of repentance for the person who experiences them. We often find suffering, loneliness, and abandonment on the paths along which divine providence leads us. All this is penance, although we should always remember that penance does not mean only punishment but that first and foremost it means conversion.

When I see into the souls of those brothers and sisters who are suffering (and I try to devote as much time as I can to them), I realize how great the truth about the baptism of repentance is, understood mainly as conversion and discovery of God. Indeed, many people rediscover God more in suffering than they had previously done in other circumstances. Experience with the sick and abandoned has brought me to the conclusion that, in suffering, the baptism of repentance becomes the baptism of revelation and grace.

But is this so for them alone? No, my dear brothers and sisters, not just for them! Although the experience of suffering and the baptism of repentance constitute a unity, they are above all a common good, because in the eternal plan of God our Father, all of us in Christ form the spiritual community that Saint Paul often described as the mystical body of Christ. This is why the individual path of penance and suffering along which the sick, the suffering, and the disenfranchised travel, transforms the baptism of repentance into the baptism of revelation and grace not only for them but for the whole parish community and for the entire Church.

My dear ones, I firmly believe this, and I act accordingly in my life and in my pastoral work. If someone asked me on what I based my pastoral work as archbishop of Krakow, I would say that to a great extent I base it on the fact that the suffering and the baptism of repentance experienced by so many of our brothers and sisters belong to the whole Church; as Jesus taught us, they are of great value.

Suffering, which is in itself an evil, becomes a good through and in Christ. The baptism of repentance proclaimed by John is transformed today into the baptism of revelation and grace brought to us by Christ.

My dear brothers and sisters, this is what I wanted to talk to you about in the course of our meeting today, and I am happy to have been able to do this during the Christmas season and at the beginning of this new year of 1969. These words contain consolation and strength for all of us. However, I know what can sometimes make you suffer most: the questions "Does anyone need me?" and "What's the purpose of all this?" This is why I want to express my deep conviction that we have great need of you and that your baptism of repentance becomes the baptism of revelation and grace and that your penance provides a foundation for the whole Church and the whole people of God.

Apart from this, Christ himself took on sufferings which marked him not only outwardly, but also inwardly. In the garden of Gethsemane and while he was in agony on the cross, he also left us examples of spiritual abandonment. Remember that you resemble him and also that we draw strength for this by sharing in your suffering.

May the baptism of repentance be the source of good, particularly for the parish of Zakopane and for all the pastoral work and efforts carried out in order to strengthen the Kingdom of God within people's souls. Help your clergy and your bishop to give fresh strength to the Kingdom of God on earth through that baptism of repentance. Accept it with serenity according to your strength, and transform it, in your life and ours, into the baptism of revelation and divine grace in order to contribute to the fulfillment of the Kingdom of God within souls. This is why you are so very necessary and so very precious! And I wanted to tell you this on this particular feast day.

My dear ones, you are part of the parish family that is the family of God and that loves you. It draws great benefit from your presence, but it also wants to give you everything it can. In this way the parish family follows the example of the Holy Family of Nazareth, which, for our salvation, gives us the Son of God for this baptism of revelation and grace.

12 January 1969

17

⚜

The Octave of Prayer
for Christian Unity

We here in the Archdiocese of Krakow are part of the Church and of Christianity, and our prayers for Christian unity are also part of all the prayers that Christians have offered up to the throne of God this week.

These prayers (ours and those of the whole Church and all Christendom) have, on the one hand, a penitential character, in that we ask God, One in the Holy Trinity, and Christ to forgive us for our divisions. On the other hand, they are also supplication, in that we take refuge in Christ's grace and ask that we may once more be united. This is the orientation and substance of the whole octave.

I am very happy that this year more of you than ever before have answered the call to pray for the noble cause of unity; indeed, the Krakow Church has never been as full as it has been in this period. The power of prayer increases in proportion to our numbers, inasmuch as the more of us there are, the more we pray, and hence the more we can hope that our prayer will be answered.

The growth of prayer for Christian unity is the fruit above all of the activity of recent popes in this field. It is certainly a reflection of the enlightened and love-filled spirit that lived among us in the person of John XXIII. Like all of Christendom, the Church is grateful to him for his great efforts in this cause. He ushered in the ecumenical era of the Church, creating the Secretariat for Christian

Unity; and when he convened the Second Vatican Council, among the tasks he gave it was the ecumenical one of working for Christian unity. John XXIII intended the Second Vatican Council to have a twofold character and to be both pastoral and ecumenical—and this was in fact the case.

However, our keen participation in great numbers in this week of prayer for Christian unity is also the fruit of Paul VI's activity, humility, and great love for Christ as living in the Church. When the pope opened the second session of the Council, we heard him speak of the divisions between Christians, and his words echoed among all Christians. These words were full of deep humility and, as the successor of Peter, he also admitted the responsibility of Catholics in contributing to the formation and continuation of divisions between Christians. Then in recent weeks we have seen him as a pilgrim in the land of Christ, moving along the Via Dolorosa in Jerusalem. We have understood the significance of this pilgrimage: he traveled to the source of Christianity and the cradle of the Church with the hope—or, better, the conviction—that only by going back to the origins of the Church can we find unity today.

We made the intentions of that pilgrimage our own and followed it with the same attitude and sentiments as those with which we followed the last moments of the earthly life of John XXIII, who in his death offered his life for the Council and for Christian unity. As I said, our prayer this week springs from the luminous rays shed by these wide-reaching actions on the part of John XXIII and Paul VI.

I should now like to explain in greater detail the questions of ecumenism and Christian unity in the thought of Vatican II. In accordance with the wishes of John XXIII, the Council allocated time to consider this serious subject.

At the first session, which took place in the fall of 1962, we examined the *schema* or draft text which was titled *Ut unum sint* (Latin words that are taken from the prayer of Jesus Christ at the Last Supper as found in Saint John's Gospel and that mean "That they may be one"). However, the discussion of this *schema* prepared for the first session of the Council threw its various defects into relief, so that the document was judged inadequate.

At the second session, therefore, held in the fall of 1963, we examined a new *schema*, which bore the more courageous title of *De Ecumenismo* (On Ecumenism). Although this is a difficult word to translate, it is now understood by everybody in its overall meaning. The new *schema* had taken into consideration the various comments made during the course of the first session. Most important, it contained a complete list of the churches, sects, and groups into which our separated brethren were divided; in previous discussions of this subject, only our Eastern brethren had been taken into account, while the Western Christian churches which had been separated from Catholicism since the sixteenth century were ignored.

This new *schema*, however, considered both groups: first, our separated Eastern brethren, the Orthodox, and, secondly, our separated Western brethren, usually described under the single heading of "Protestants."

Apart from this, in response to requests made at the previous session of the Council, the new *schema* gives practical details of what must be done regarding ecumenism on the Catholic side. Lastly, it gives a number of suggestions and practical recommendations as to how ecumenism can be put into practice. I have here the second part of the *schema*, and I should like to read you at least the titles of the main paragraphs because they define more clearly precisely how we must move towards unification:

"De interiore Ecclesiae renovatione"—which means that the Church itself must work towards interior renewal.

"De conversione cordis"—all of us, both Christians and non-Christians, but especially we Catholics, must be converted.

"De sanctitate vitae"—we must be outstanding for the holiness of our lives.

"De oratione unanimi"—we must pray together for Christian unity.

"De fratrum mutua cognitione"—we Catholics and our separated brethren must learn to know one another.

"De instructione ecumenica"—which means that in teaching the truths of the faith, whether to future priests in seminaries, or to the laity, we must place proper emphasis on the questions of ecumenism.

"De modo exsponendi et exsprimendi doctrinam fidei"—we must proclaim the truths of the faith in their fullness, while always being very careful to emphasize those aspects that unite us rather than those that divide us.

"De cooperatione cum fratribus separatis"—we must work together with our separated brethren in every area we can (and there are many of these).

This new *schema* was accepted, and there was animated and fruitful discussion of it during the session last fall. A major part in this discussion was played by bishops from countries such as Holland, Germany, and the United States, where Catholics are in a minority or where they represent about half the population while our separated brethren make up a considerable part of the rest.

Many Eastern bishops, who have firsthand knowledge of the problems of our separated Eastern brethren, took part in this discussion; and this applies to the Polish bishops too. The *schema* was also enriched by two sections which have yet to be discussed. The first, "De Iudeis," considers the chosen people of the Old Testament, whereas the other, which is of great importance for Christian ecumenism, bears the title "De libertate religiosa" and concerns religious freedom.

I have described to you how the Council has been approaching the ecumenical question, so that you can see that the Church is not dealing with it simply in theory but is deeply concerned with it on a practical level too.

All of us who were there felt the warm, ecumenical atmosphere in the Council meetings, both during the first session when the bishops were very careful not to place obstacles in the way of reconciliation with our separated brethren and also in the second session when we considered together the best ways to move toward reunification.

I should now like to draw some conclusions. After the first and second sessions, I would describe the present situation of the ecumenical question as follows: all Christians, both Catholics and our separated brethren in the East and in the West, must draw closer to one another while retaining our present specific characteristics.

This is an important step forward because previously we believed that it would be impossible to draw closer in any way if we all remained as we are now.

This is the situation at present. We still remember vividly the kiss of peace exchanged in Jerusalem by Paul VI and the Patriarch Athenagoras of Constantinople. However, while this is the present situation, the future must be considered. Ecumenism must develop since it is not simply a matter of Christians drawing closer to one another but above all of their reunification.

What is the future of ecumenism and its more universal prospects, which lie not only in the hands of God but also in ours? It means bringing about Christian unity while looking back to the origins of Christianity and the Church. We cannot be united with one another on the basis of any compromise!

The Church is not only a collection of people who tolerate one another. The Church of Christ is an organic unity, or body—the mystical body of Christ. However, the mystical unity of this body also entails the social unity on a practical level of the whole people of God—a people that must gradually grow and develop to its full maturity.

So these are the ecumenical prospects in both the short and long term. These prospects are known to God in whose all-seeing mind the future is already a reality, but it is up to us to move toward them although we cannot know how long this will take.

I have told you what means and methods the Council has indicated for furthering the cause of reunification. But do we understand what they really entail? They mean that as Christians (and especially as Catholics) we must slowly but surely cooperate with divine grace, which alone makes reunification a possibility. And we can depend on the fruits of grace, so that we must always be as open as possible to the different ways in which it works. My dear ones, the whole question of division has very deep roots within human nature—in our mind, will, and heart. These roots are in fact so deep that without the assistance of divine grace it is impossible for us to eliminate them, however hard we try.

There are other aspects of this question, since Christian unity is not simply an internal matter, concerning only the Church and Christianity, or an issue regarding the various confessions and churches. No, my dear ones, in a certain sense it is a much broader question, the solution of which has ramifications for all humanity. If we Christians were able to settle our differences and be reunited with one another, this would set a wonderful example of optimism for all humanity and be a great lesson as to our real capacities as human beings. Our lives should not be founded on aggression, hatred, and opposition but on peace, union, and mutual understanding by discovering what we have in common. So when we pray for Christian unity, we are at the same time praying for a major problem of all those who are outside the Church and are not Christians but who (believe me) look to us with hope; they probably do not say so in so many words, but they feel it just the same.

Unity is a development called for in the gospel and entails a gradual but deep recognition of the gospel truths. Its fulfillment is a great work of grace, but also a great human work when, united with Christ, we act under the inspiration of grace.

These are the broader prospects (and their deeper implications) for which we have been praying this week in this Dominican church. Christian unity should be a true force in enabling Christ and the gospel to touch human souls. God manifests himself in such unity, as Christ taught us when he prayed for the unity of his disciples: "That they may all be one, even as you, Father, are in me, and I in you" (John 17:1).

It is a question of the manifestation of God's unity in its highest form, which is the Holy Trinity. Through our unity—the unity of all Christians—we must be a sign and bear witness here on earth so that every person can see this unity; we must bear witness to the supernatural unity found in God himself in the Holy Trinity.

My dear ones, these are the higher prospects opened up by Christian unity, so that we have been praying for something very important this week. We must continue to pray and never stop, since prayer may be simple but it is a most effective instrument: "Ask and you shall receive" (John 16:24).

May the sacrifice of the Holy Mass, which we are now celebrating, be our shared cry of union with Christ. Let us pray that our prayer may become his, and our offering his.

May the sacrifice of the only-begotten Son of God speak for us, for the Church and for our separated brethren. May it intercede for all humanity in prayer, in supplication, and in heartfelt invocation, and may this prayer be answered through the grace and mercy of God, who is One and Three.

25 January 1964

*　　*　　*

We always listen with great attention (indeed, I would say, with great emotion) to that reading from the Acts of the Apostles which tells us of Saint Paul's conversion (9:1–30). It is a quite extraordinary and significant event, especially if we bear in mind its general context and the fact that it took place just outside the gates of Damascus.

Saul of Tarsus, the persecutor of that Church of God that had been formed by Christ's apostles in Jerusalem, was converted to Christ and his Church. He had been persecuting the Church because of his deep-felt conviction that the truth was to be found only in the Old Testament and that the new one was therefore still to come. He had denied Christ but was now converted to him, after himself encountering Christ.

Christ, the risen One, who had ascended to sit at the right hand of the Father, came back once more in order to convert Saul of Tarsus and make him an apostle. And suddenly Saul underwent an interior revolution and broke completely with his past. He would hold throughout the rest of his life to what he now accepted and confessed—right up to his last breath and his martyrdom.

This transformation within an individual is symbolic of the history of the people of God, inasmuch as the Old Testament was transcended and entered definitively into the new. The sworn enemy of the new became its supporter and witness, bringing with him the old.

However, let us go further and consider in greater depth this remarkable event but more especially its significance. The convert Saul, who would henceforth be the Apostle Paul and whose conversion was unique and unrepeatable, became the source of a new orientation in the Church and in the history of the people of God, and it is to him that we owe that basic transformation in the work of evangelization. While the other apostles, including Peter, felt they were bound to the laws of the chosen people when proclaiming the New Covenant, Paul openly brought the gospel to the pagans— and this is why Christ described him as his "chosen instrument" (Acts 9:15). We can see this great change of direction in the proclamation of the gospel and in the history of the people of God on earth as a fruit of Saint Paul's conversion.

Today, following the liturgical calendar, we reflect on this conversion, and we should try and see all the consequences and fruits of this event. This reflection will lend deeper meaning to the prayer that we rightly offer up today for Christian unity.

We pray for Christian unity, but, as today's liturgy clearly shows, this unity must mean conversion. Every Christian needs conversion. But, we may ask, to whom must they be converted? Maybe to one another? Yes, certainly. However, before this can take place, they must first be converted to Christ, who prayed: "That they may all be one, even as you, Father, are in me, and I in you" (John 17:21). On the occasion of the celebration of Saint Paul's conversion, prayer for the unity of Christians is also prayer for their conversion to that unity that was indicated by Christ.

Christ is one. His physical body is one, and his mystical body—in other words, the Church—must also be one. Within himself, Christ, who is one, wants to indicate the unity of Christians. However, since even in the upper room he already knew about the separations and divisions which would threaten this unity, he earnestly prayed "that they may all be one."

I believe that the greatest step forward by Christianity in the twentieth century—and particularly by the Second Vatican Council, which is rightly called an ecumenical council—has been the realization of the method to be used in working towards unity. This method is very simple although unfortunately for centuries it was not clearly enough understood in our consciences and hearts. For almost a thousand years it had been thought that the unity of Christians and of the whole Church meant institutional unification.

The Second Vatican Council has helped us to reach a deeper understanding of the mystery of the Church, so that we see Christ in it, living in the unity of his mystical life and mystical body; and we have come to realize that the unity of Christians means first and foremost universal conversion to Christ, who prayed "that they may all be one." This is the method or ecumenical formula rediscovered by the Council and by contemporary Christians. Conversion is the basis of our prayer for Christian unity.

Saint Paul's conversion provides us with a model for the conversion through which all the Christians in the world must pass if they are to carry out the will of their Master that they all be one. When Popes John XXIII and Paul VI spoke on this subject at the beginning of the different sessions of the Council, they expressed themselves with great humility, since humility is necessary in anyone placing himself in an attitude of conversion. Emphasizing this humility, Paul VI wanted and wants to be the first Christian to draw all Christendom to conversion, thus leading it to unity.

My dear ones, there are many of us here; let us all gather around the altar in prayer. Our Lord Jesus was the first to pray for unity and showed us the way to conversion and hence to Christian unity.

When we gather around this altar today, we are imitating Christ in his prayer. Our prayer is the prayer of many people, but it is one prayer; it is the prayer of all of us, but it is one in Christ. In all Catholic and other Christian churches hundreds of millions of voices are being raised in one single prayer, which echoes the prayer of Christ and unites us in the one Christ.

And now, my dear ones, as we move on to the part of the holy sacrifice which is called the Eucharist, to the consecration and communion, let us bring our individual prayers to Christ for his intercession. In this sacrifice, which again renews the sacrifice of the cross, we shall hear Christ himself praying: "That they may all be one, Father, as you are in me, and I in you."

25 January 1966

* * *

We have gathered here, as we do each year, to reflect on the conversion of Saint Paul; the Church sets aside a special day of the liturgical year for its celebration.

This event took place under the walls of Damascus and was described in the Acts of the Apostles as we have just heard. It was also recalled by Saint Paul himself in some of his letters, which provide us with important personal insights into what Saul of Tarsus, who later became Paul, experienced under the walls of Damascus.

When he was still known as Saul, he was quite a different person and rejected Jesus Christ. Then, from the moment he was called, Paul accepted Jesus Christ and identified himself with him. We should reflect carefully on this event; its significance is mainly interior, in that it happened within this man's soul, within his conscience, will, and heart.

Prior to this Saul had rejected Jesus Christ with great vehemence and without mercy, just as the other Pharisees (of whom he was one) did. The Pharisees had rejected Christ and his teachings and miracles so strongly that they had brought him before the Roman governor, Pontius Pilate, in order to have him condemned to death. They had rejected him pitilessly and harshly and had viewed his death on the cross as a fitting epilogue to their maneuvers. Saul rejected Christ in the same vehement and pitiless way, as we have just heard, and was on his way from Jerusalem to Damascus in order to pursue the persecution of those who had accepted Jesus.

Now we see this same Saul accepting Christ against whom he had previously so strongly fought. He accepted him as soon as he became aware, like the other disciples and apostles, that Jesus was still alive. We know that after the resurrection Jesus appeared to his apostles in various places and under various circumstances. He appeared to Saul under the gates of Damascus, and it was then that Saul accepted Jesus. He now accepted him just as passionately as he had previously rejected him.

Jesus Christ can be recognized in the soul of Paul even more clearly than in most of his disicples. All Saint Paul's letters bear witness to this; they constitute the best commentary on his conversion and demonstrate how deep it must have been. The sentence which best expresses this is, "It is no longer I who live, but Christ who lives in me" (Galatians 2:20), which shows just how profoundly he accepted and welcomed Jesus Christ.

Each year the Church meditates afresh on Saint Paul's conversion, and it does so, as the celebrant reminded us at the beginning, in order that we too may continue to be converted. Each of us must reflect on Saul's conversion beneath the walls of Damascus and on his transformation from persecutor into apostle in order to develop our own conversion, since we have constant need of this. Although we cannot expect events like the one which took place outside Damascus, we must undergo constant conversion, and our conversion must be measured and evaluated against the same criteria: How far have I rejected Christ in the past? To what extent have I now accepted him? How clearly can he be seen in me?

These criteria may sound a bit radical, and maybe nobody present would want to confess that at some point in his life he rejected Jesus Christ. However, if we move on to the second and third questions—"To what extent have I now accepted him?" and "How clearly can he be seen in me?"—we realize how immense perfection is and how much we need constant conversion to be able to say, with Saint Paul: "It is no longer I who live, but Christ who lives in me." We can then see how much we must ask of ourselves if we are to consider ourselves Christians.

In a number of ways the period in which we are living is like the early days of Christianity. Although, so far as can be seen, we do not have the sort of persecutions which took place under the Roman Empire, Jesus Christ is being similarly rejected, even if this may not be stated openly. After two thousand years a whole new series of ways of rejecting Christ has been worked out. He is, for instance, rejected when people claim that the only true human aspiration is that of reaching what they call a scientific view of the world—while no mention is made of the fact that a large number of true scientists do accept Christ. So what is the reason for such a misleading statement? The secularization of public life is planned in the name of progress and humanism. At first glance there seems to be nothing here that rejects Christ, but we know that such a rejection is contemplated; we know that as a result of this plan his sign—the cross—will no longer be found in any public building.* This is the sort of result "progress" and "secularization" tend to bring.

This is how Jesus Christ is rejected today, and there are various different systems and formulations for putting this into practice. Jesus Christ is rejected, as he was in Jerusalem where he was crucified and as he was later under the Roman Empire in the period of the persecutions.

However, what is wonderful is that the more deep-rooted, pitiless, and oppressive this attitude is, the more we hear about conversion to Jesus Christ! Here we find a reflection of the mystery of Paul. Conversion increases wherever Christ is most violently rejected. This also happens because wherever Christ is cruelly rejected without any respect for the rights of the human heart and conscience, people react and turn to Jesus Christ, who thus becomes—as he has been in the past—the symbol of the most fundamental human aspirations and most elementary human rights.

Saint Paul himself pointed out that Christ has set us free and wrote about this freedom (Galatians 5). We know that under the attack of atheism, which does not bother about human freedom and which creates social oppression, people react against all this and turn to Jesus Christ. Atheism leads not only individuals but whole societies to conversion because only Christ can bring us to freedom. He had complete interior freedom, even to the extent of choosing the cross, so that he came to bring freedom to humanity and to each individual who has been deprived of it or is suffering from repression or is being officially urged to reject Christ. He came in order that people might regain freedom and hence human dignity, so that in this dignity they might rediscover that God who has spoken to us through Jesus Christ and who has shown us unlimited love in him.

---

*In many Catholic countries a crucifix is found in each classroom, law court, etc.

Although the age in which we are living may not outwardly resemble that of Saul of Tarsus, who then became Paul the Apostle, it does provide us with opportunities and clues for understanding and appreciating his conversion and sharing in it.

On this feast day I also want to offer my warmest good wishes to the Father Visitator of the Polish Province of the Congregation of the Fathers of the Mission*, for the whole of their community which performs such admirable work both in this country and also among our Polish emigrants. I saw the good work you are doing in the United States, and I know that members of this province are also active in other places. I want to draw particular attention to the good work they are doing here in Krakow in preparing candidates for the priesthood in their own seminary and in cooperating with the Institute of Theology.

While we are praying together with those who have gathered here for the eucharistic liturgy today, I want to express my fervent hope that your activity, which has been continuing now for some generations, may continue to develop under the patronage of Saint Paul, who teaches us that we must accept Christ, even if we have previously rejected him, and also how to reach the point at which we can state with the Apostle to the Gentiles: "It is no longer I who live, but Christ who lives in me."

25 January 977

*   *   *

"Let every tongue confess that Jesus Christ is Lord, to the glory of God the Father."

With these words, our Krakow church joins its prayers and supplications to those of the universal Church in this octave of prayer for Christian unity. Together with the rest of the Church, we pray for Christian unity in the hope and trust that through it "every tongue may confess that Jesus Christ is Lord."

Prayer for Christian unity has special meaning this year because, as you know, we are celebrating Holy Year in our archdiocese—as is

---

*The Vincentian Fathers

the case throughout Poland and everywhere else in the world, except for Rome. Holy Year is celebrated every twenty-five years. Although this ancient tradition of the Church has its basis in the Old Testament, it springs above all from the need to offer special worship on earth to our Lord and Spouse, Jesus Christ.

In its present jubilee form, this tradition began in the Middle Ages and has demonstrated through the centuries how the Church seeks Christ and is constantly converted to him, moving forward with its eyes on him. Christ is the Alpha and Omega—the beginning and the end—of human history but first and foremost of the history of the people of God on this earth. He is the Alpha and Omega of the history of the Church.

In accordance with this ancient tradition, ten years after the Second Vatican Council the Holy Father Paul VI proclaimed 1975 as Holy Year while recommending that it should be celebrated one year earlier everywhere except in Rome. The Holy Father wanted to further the cause of reconciliation in this way. Thus this Holy Year has an ecumenical character, which is why the prayers for Christian unity which we offer now and in the future are of special importance. During this octave we pray in a special way for the reconciliation of Christians. We should, however, consider what type of reconciliation is intended. Reconciliation should in the first place be taken in the sense in which it is used by the Second Vatican Council. Although the theme of reconciliation runs through most of the Council teachings, it is dealt with more specifically in the Dogmatic Constitution on the Church (*Lumen gentium*) and in the Decree on Ecumenism (*Unitatis redintegratio*).

However, the Council is not our only point of reference. We seek the reconciliation described by the Apostle Paul in his first letter to the Corinthians which we have just heard in the liturgy of the word. Saint Paul speaks of the resemblance between the Church and the human body. The human body is made up of various organs and cells, which form one single body animated by one single spirit. The Church makes up the mystical body of Jesus Christ, precisely because it is animated by one single Spirit—the Spirit of Jesus Christ, who is the Holy Spirit. The Spirit is thus the foundation of unity, inasmuch as he makes the mystical body of Christ one. We can therefore understand why, when the Holy Father announced this Holy Year, he specifically referred to the Holy Spirit as the foundation of unity and reconciliation, saying that we must turn to him so that everything that is divided and torn may be reunited and reconciled. We are sure that the faith of the Apostle Paul inspires not only us but also our brethren who may be institutionally separated from us but who are spiritually united to us through Jesus Christ. We should at least remember that basic unity which springs from baptism—as the Apostle Paul pointed out to the Corinthians.

Thus, even if they have been divided for centuries, all Christians who have been baptized in Christ Jesus have every right to trust that the Holy Spirit, who is the basis of unity, will act in them and bring them all into full communion in the Church of Christ.

We confess this faith today together with the whole of the Church, so that it is like a light pervading our common, ecumenical prayer. Together with all Christians, the church in Krakow also prays for the fulfillment of what Christ prayed to the Father for in the upper room, thinking of those who would come after him over the centuries: "That they may all be one, Father." We make this prayer our own. It represents a reproach to us for not being united as Christ wanted; however, it is also a call full of the hope that we shall gradually be able to create this unity.

We want to contribute to this unity, first of all with prayer but also through fraternal contacts with other Christians. Such meetings are already taking place in Krakow and are gradually becoming more widespread and effective, despite the many difficulties involved. We meet one another and talk together not only during this special week but also on various other occasions. The pastoral synod that is at present being held in our archdiocese is also working in this area; we want to understand the exact situation regarding ecumenism today—how much Christian unity has been achieved in the past, what form it could take today, and what we can do to help bring it about. The stated objective of the synod, which began its work about two years ago, is the implementation of the teachings of the Second Vatican Council in the Archdiocese of Krakow; and since one of the many tasks the Council set the whole Church is that of unity among all Christians, we too want to work towards this aim as effectively as possible.

Today we bring the work of the synod and also our many meetings and contacts with our Christian brothers who are separated from the Catholic Church to the altar as our offering. This gift is clearly neither perfect nor yet fully mature; however, it is in constant development. With each year we develop it, and each year we bring it to this altar with the hope that through prayer and sacrifice our offering may constantly grow and bring us ever closer to Christian unity in accordance with the thought and will of Jesus Christ.

May all our efforts, my dear brothers and sisters—including those who are still separated from us but who are especially dear to our hearts—fulfill our prayer that every tongue may confess that Jesus Christ is Lord.

Our Lord Jesus Christ comes to us under the species of bread and wine in order to nourish our souls, and in the Holy Spirit he becomes the source of life and unity. As we celebrate the Holy Mass, we shall welcome him into our hearts with fervent prayer and with the great hope that through the mystery of his body and blood that wonderful unity in the Holy Spirit may grow in us—that unity which Jesus Christ desires for every age and for all time.

After reflecting on the word of God, we draw near to the altar in faith, in order to celebrate the Eucharist; this faith goes hand in hand with veneration, love, and hope.

27 January 1974

* * *

On a mountainside in Galilee that had been indicated to them, the eleven disciples listened to and absorbed the Master's words, message and instructions: "Go therefore and make disciples of all nations, baptizing them in the name of the Father and of the Son and of the Holy Spirit, teaching them to observe all that I have commanded you; and lo, I am with you always, to the close of the age" (Matthew 28:19–20).

These words were also reflected on by the World Conference of Bishops in the course of the recent synod which met to discuss evangelization in the modern world. Today, as in the past, these words set us the same task of evangelizing the world, and we who took part in the synod realized how important and urgent this is. We meditated on these words, discussing them and exchanging experiences, in order to prepare ourselves inwardly to carry out this same task today.

We undertook this work in an ecumenical spirit, bearing in mind the Second Vatican Council, the witness of life of our late beloved Pope John XXIII, who was such a providential figure, and the conciliar Decree on Ecumenism. This is why Christians belonging to separated communities and churches were also invited to the synod. Their presence and participation showed us how much, despite separation, they are becoming steadily more imbued with the sense of unity represented by God himself. The Second Vatican Council reminded us of this, pointing out that the Church means the unity of the people of God, founded on the supreme communion of Father, Son, and Holy Spirit. This undeniable truth was the source of our desire to give human form to the divine unity of the Church of Christ.

The representatives of the separated communities and churches also told us how they view the evangelization of the modern world. Although the secretary general of the World Council of Churches belongs to a separated Church, his very moving address showed us how much he loves the gospel and how united he is with us over the question of evangelization. This led us to realize that it is the separation of Christians and their division into different communities and churches which makes our task more difficult, which in turn increases the need we feel for unity. The need for Christian unity in fact springs from evangelization, inasmuch as those to whom we bring Christ's truth expect to see his gospel and words being followed, among them the prayer he spoke on the eve of his Passion: "That they may all be one, even as you, Father, are in me, and I in you" (John 17:21).

The people we go out to evangelize look to us for unity, and we must therefore work towards it. We realized this even more clearly during the synod of bishops, and I felt it particularly strongly at our meeting with the representatives of the World Council of Churches.

Today we have met together to pray as we do each year. What can I say to you at the end of this solemn octave in which we have gathered together in the venerable church of the Dominican Fathers? I can observe that this week of prayer for Christian unity is being taken more and more seriously. At different meetings in the Archdiocese of Krakow, I have heard and seen that unity is being prayed for constantly in every parish.

We have taken to heart the instructions of the Second Vatican Council and seen the significance of the new orientation in the history of the Church providentially initiated by Pope John XXIII. It means moving on from investigations of the truth of individual churches to praying for unity in the truth, in the awareness that the path to unity in the truth is that of love. So we must look for everything that unites us, for this is the law of love. We are confident that this attitude will gradually lead to that unity in the truth of the faith for which we are all working.

We draw this confidence from the view of the Church given us by Saint Paul, which constitutes an intangible source of faith and life. The words chosen this year as the theme for Christian unity week also refer to this view: Christ is the head of the Church, and the Church is his body. Although this body is human and has thus been torn apart and divided over the centuries, its head, Jesus Christ, represents its true unity. We cannot believe that the Church will always be divided when Christ, the head of his body, is one. Unity will be regained in the living strength which flows from the head to the body.

We pray that all may be made new in Christ, who is the head of the Church; that all the links that bind the individual cells together into the organism may be reconstituted; and that this organism may live with one single life.

This is the source of our unshakable hope, despite the present difficulties which threaten faith, religion, and Christianity. Although Christians may be separated and belong to different communities and churches, they all have Christ as their one head and reunited in him they can rediscover social and ecclesial unity. This is our hope, and it is not a vain one.

Now that we have started on this path of hope together with our separated brethren (to whom I should like to express my warmest greetings), we look with unshakable faith to Christ as our head. His Spirit will help us to carry out what is impossible for men to do alone. May the gift of unity in the Holy Spirit be with us all; this is the desire which, linked with goodwill, we place as our offering on this altar.

Let us pray that all the people of God on earth may share more and more each year in the unity of the Father, Son and Holy Spirit.

26 January 1975

* * *

Today we bring to a conclusion the octave of prayer for unity in which all Christians have meditated on the meaning of a brief phrase from Saint Paul's first letter to the Corinthians: "We are God's fellow workers" (3:9).

If we reflect on the inner meaning of this phrase, we must realize that it cannot refer only to us. And this is a good thing because we would otherwise be forced to admit that we are not God's fellow workers. Although as Christians we acknowledge God and say that we are his servants and assistants, we frequently act as obstacles to his work, inasmuch as we know that God is love and unity and that he expects unity in truth and love from us, but we pay no attention to his wishes in this regard. Therefore if we think that the statement that we are God's fellow workers refers only to us, we must conclude that we are either unfaithful or in error.

However, when Saint Paul calls us to meditate on these words and put them into effect, he tells us not to think of ourselves but of Christ. We are God's fellow workers in Christ and thanks to Christ. Christ is one not only in the historical sense, but also in the mystical sense. There is only one single, mystical Christ, one single, mystical body of Christ in which we are all united as cells of one great spiritual organism who all help one another. In this wonderful, spiritual organism we are all God's fellow workers.

In the course of this week of prayer for Christian unity we have meditated on Saint Paul's words, and today we bring the week to a close with them. Let us reflect once more on who we are as Christians, as members of the people of God—on who we are in God's mind and plans, on who we are in Christ.

And although we may be separated socially and institutionally, the knowledge that we are united in Christ and as such are God's fellow workers is of consolation to us and encourages our hope for the future.

Saint Paul's words must be heard not only as a statement but also as a call to us as modern-day Christians, so that Saint Paul's "we are" becomes "we must be." "We must be God's fellow workers," which means that we must seek that unity which unites us in Christ, and that we must seek it despite any divisions. As twentieth-century Christians and as Catholics in this era of the Second Vatican Council, this is how we must take these words. We know that that unity which we lack does exist, and we are confident that we shall mature and develop until it is brought about.

The unity which is in Christ must find its communitarian expression in the Church. We are called to be God's fellow workers, so that the Church, as the outward manifestation of the unity that, through Christ, links men to God in the Holy Trinity, may work with God in the world throughout the history of the vast human family.

My dear brothers and sisters, these are the thoughts on which we have concentrated in the course of this octave. These thoughts of themselves constitute a prayer—or, to be exact, they are easily transformed into prayer. This week the whole Church, with all the individual churches and Christian communities, has reflected on the simple words of Saint Paul and transformed them into a prayer: "May we all be God's fellow workers." This prayer has been made with great humility, because of the awareness that we are not united, as Christ wants, but divided. Even so, our prayer contains great hope. Hope indicates a desire and points toward fulfillment. Our desire is that the Church may come to manifest the unity we have in God's mind and in Christ—the unity which filled Christ's heart at the Last Supper, when he prayed to his Father: "That they may all be one, even as you, Father, are in me, and I in you" (John 17:21).

In a certain way our prayer also becomes a continuation of Christ's. We want to be one; we desire the unity which we have in God's intentions and in the mystical Christ; and we want to be the full expression of this desire so as to be able to work with God toward the fulfillment of his plan of glory and peace. We are reminded of the words of the hymn: "Glory to God in the highest, and peace on earth to men of goodwill." Jesus calls us all to be fellow workers with God in the work of divine glory and in the work of peace, love, and justice, in the broadest possible sense.

We have prayed for this in the course of the week. And today too I want you to pray for it with me. My dear brothers and sisters, please pray with me before the altar, as Christ prayed in the upper room "that they may all be one," and that in this unity we may become God's fellow workers in Christ's vast work of salvation. Wherever Christ works—in Bethlehem, in the upper room, on the cross—he is one, so that we can play a more and more effective part in this work of salvation.

We come to this altar each year with these prayers. And each year we look to the future, to the moment when, through God's mercy, Christians will be united and, before the eyes of all humanity, there will be (to use Christ's words) "one flock, one Shepherd" (John 10:16).

25 January 1970